OTHER PUBLICATIONS FROM THE DRUCKER FOUNDATION

Organizational Leadership Resource

The Drucker Foundation Self-Assessment Tool

The Drucker Foundation Future Series

The Leader of the Future, *Frances Hesselbein, Marshall Goldsmith, Richard Beckhard, Editors*

The Organization of the Future, *Frances Hesselbein, Marshall Goldsmith, Richard Beckhard, Editors*

The Community of the Future, *Frances Hesselbein, Marshall Goldsmith, Richard Beckhard, Richard F. Schubert, Editors*

Wisdom to Action Series

Leading for Innovation, *Frances Hesselbein, Marshall Goldsmith, Iain Somerville, Editors*

Leading Beyond the Walls, *Frances Hesselbein, Marshall Goldsmith, Iain Somerville, Editors*

Leaderbooks

The Collaboration Challenge: How Nonprofits and Businesses Succeed Through Strategic Alliances, *James E. Austin*

Meeting the Collaboration Challenge (workbook and video)

Journal and Related Books

Leader to Leader Journal

Leader to Leader: Enduring Insights on Leadership from the Drucker Foundation's Award-Winning Journal, *Frances Hesselbein, Paul Cohen, Editors*

On High-Performance Organizations, *Frances Hesselbein, Rob Johnston, Editors*

On Leading Change, *Frances Hesselbein, Rob Johnston, Editors*

On Mission and Leadership, *Frances Hesselbein, Rob Johnston, Editors*

Video Training Resources

Excellence in Nonprofit Leadership Video, *featuring Peter F. Drucker, Max De Pree, Frances Hesselbein, and Michele Hunt. Moderated by Richard F. Schubert*

Leading in a Time of Change: What It Will Take to Lead Tomorrow, *a conversation with Peter F. Drucker and Peter M. Senge, introduction by Frances Hesselbein*

Lessons in Leadership Video, *with Peter F. Drucker*

Online Resources

www.drucker.org

On Creativity, Innovation, and Renewal

**A DRUCKER FOUNDATION
LEADERBOOK**

ABOUT THE DRUCKER FOUNDATION

The Peter F. Drucker Foundation for Nonprofit Management, founded in 1990, takes its name and inspiration from the acknowledged father of modern management. By providing educational opportunities and resources, the foundation furthers its mission "to lead social sector organizations toward excellence in performance." It pursues this mission through the presentation of conferences, video teleconferences, the annual Peter F. Drucker Award for Nonprofit Innovation, and the annual Frances Hesselbein Community Innovation Fellows Program, as well as through the development of management resources, partnerships, and publications.

The Drucker Foundation believes that a healthy society requires three vital sectors: a public sector of effective governments, a private sector of effective businesses, and a social sector of effective community organizations. The mission of the social sector and its organizations is to change lives. It accomplishes this mission by addressing the needs of the spirit, mind, and body of individuals, the community, and society. This sector and its organizations also create a meaningful sphere of effective and responsible citizenship.

In the ten years after its inception, the Drucker Foundation, among other things:

- Presented the Drucker Innovation Award, which each year generates hundreds of applications from local community enterprises; many applicants work in fields in which results are difficult to achieve
- Worked with social sector leaders through the Frances Hesselbein Community Innovation Fellows program
- Held more than twenty conferences in the United States and in countries around the world
- Developed thirteen books: the *Self-Assessment Tool* (revised 1998), for nonprofit organizations; three books in the Drucker Foundation Future Series, *The Leader of the Future* (1996), *The Organization of the Future* (1997), and *The Community of the Future* (1998); *Leader to Leader* (1999); *Leading Beyond the Walls* (1999); *The Collaboration Challenge* (2000); the *Leading in a Time of Change* viewer's workbook and video (2001); *Leading for Innovation* (2002); and *On Mission and Leadership*, *On Leading Change*, *On High-Performance Organizations*, and *On Creativity, Innovation, and Renewal* (all 2002)
- Developed *Leader to Leader*, a quarterly journal for leaders from all three sectors
- Established a Web site (drucker.org) that shares articles on leadership and management and examples of nonprofit innovation with hundreds of thousands of visitors each year

For more information on the Drucker Foundation, contact:

The Peter F. Drucker Foundation for Nonprofit Management
320 Park Avenue, Third Floor, New York, NY 10022-6839 U.S.A.
Telephone: (212) 224-1174 • Fax: (212) 224-2508
E-mail: info@pfdf.org • Web address: www.drucker.org

On Creativity, Innovation, and Renewal

A LEADER TO LEADER GUIDE

Frances Hesselbein
Rob Johnston
Editors

JOSSEY-BASS
A Wiley Company
www.josseybass.com

Published by

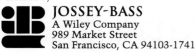 **JOSSEY-BASS**
A Wiley Company
989 Market Street
San Francisco, CA 94103-1741

www.josseybass.com

Jossey-Bass books and products are available through most bookstores. To contact Jossey-Bass directly, call (888) 378-2537, fax to (800) 605-2665, or visit our Web site at www.josseybass.com.

Substantial discounts on bulk quantities of Jossey-Bass books are available to corporations, professional associations, and other organizations. For details and discount information, contact the special sales department at Jossey-Bass.

We at Jossey-Bass strive to use the most environmentally sensitive paper stocks available to us. Our publications are printed on acid-free recycled stock whenever possible, and our paper always meets or exceeds minimum GPO and EPA requirements.

Library of Congress Cataloging-in-Publication Data

On creativity, innovation, and renewal : a leader to leader guide / Frances Hesselbein and Rob Johnston, editors.—1st ed.
    p. cm.
"Drucker Foundation Leaderbooks."
Includes index.
ISBN 0-7879-6067-5 (alk. paper)
    1. Creative ability in business. 2. Technological innovations. 3. Organizational change. I. Hesselbein, Frances. II. Johnston, Rob, date
HD53 .O526 2002
658.4—dc21   2001007586

FIRST EDITION

HB Printing 10 9 8 7 6 5 4 3 2 1

Contents

Introduction

People in the United States and around the world have an enormous hunger for ideas; that's why in 1996 the Drucker Foundation launched *Leader to Leader*, a journal of ideas by leaders for leaders. This hunger among millions of working executives demonstrates their concern for the future and commitment to making a difference.

The incisive thinkers and remarkable leaders who have contributed to the journal and its related books open doors, spark ideas, raise signal flags, and help satisfy that universal hunger. These extraordinary contributors have taught us, among other things, that great leaders do not live isolated from the world; they are engaged with and deeply care about others. They measure their own success by the real-world impact of their work. That people throughout our society and organizations want to contribute to a better world has been a major premise of *Leader to Leader*.

We learned, too, that astonishing things happen when you give intelligent, effective people a free hand. Never have we approached our authors with an assigned topic or reviewed their work before an advisory board or peer review; when you're working with the best in the world, you don't do that. Rather, we simply asked, "What's on your mind? What issues will most affect leaders, organizations, or communities in the coming years?"

From that unfettered process, several coherent themes emerged with astonishing clarity. They are evident in the four volumes of the Leader to Leader Guides. This volume, *On Creativity, Innovation, and Renewal,* explores how leaders can keep an organization changing with a focus on building the future. It explores the roles of leaders in establishing an environment that appreciates creativity and diversity, creating passion and a sense of urgency. Other issues addressed include the need to focus on the customer and the call to simultaneously build community within the organization and strengthen the organization's position in the community beyond its walls.

The other volumes in this series are *On Mission and Leadership,* which explores the essential role that mission plays in defining and supporting leadership; *On Leading Change,* which explores the challenges of bringing organizations through transformation; and *On High-Performance Organizations,* which explores getting the most from the people and other resources of each organization.

We gathered the wisdom of our contributors so that our readers could find insight and inspiration to make a difference in their organizations and their communities. We hope our collection will help you to lead, to inspire a change, to strengthen your performance, or to spark and sustain a renewal. We wish you the best as you apply these lessons to the work you do and the people you touch.

February 2002

Frances Hesselbein
Easton, Pennsylvania

Rob Johnston
New York, New York

About the Editors

Frances Hesselbein is chairman of the board of governors of the Peter F. Drucker Foundation for Nonprofit Management and is the former chief executive of the Girl Scouts of the U.S.A. She is a member of the boards of other organizations and corporations and is the lead editor of the Drucker Foundation's best-selling books, including *The Leader of the Future*, *The Organization of the Future*, *The Community of the Future*, *Leading Beyond the Walls*, and *Leader to Leader*, published by Jossey-Bass. She also serves as editor in chief of the journal *Leader to Leader*. She speaks on leadership and management to audiences around the world in the private, nonprofit, and governmental sectors. She has received fifteen honorary doctorates and was awarded the Presidential Medal of Freedom in 1998.

Rob Johnston is president and CEO of the Peter F. Drucker Foundation for Nonprofit Management. He has served the Drucker Foundation since 1991 and was appointed president effective March 2001. At the foundation he has led program development, the Drucker Innovation Award program, publication development, and teleconference and conference development.

He was executive producer for *Leading in a Time of Change*, a 2001 video featuring Peter F. Drucker and Peter M. Senge, and for *The Nonprofit Leader of the Future*, the foundation's 1997 video teleconference broadcast to 10,000 leaders across the United States. He leads the editorial development of the foundation's Web site (drucker.org) and is a senior editor for *Leader to Leader*. Johnston earned a B.A. degree in the history of art from Yale and an M.B.A. degree from Stanford. He contributed a chapter to *Enterprising Nonprofits* (John Wiley & Sons, 2001).

On Creativity, Innovation, and Renewal

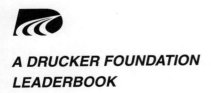

**A DRUCKER FOUNDATION
LEADERBOOK**

1

When the Roll Is Called in 2010

Frances Hesselbein

To be sustainable, an organization must scan its environment to identify major trends; review its mission and refine it to reflect changes in the environment; abandon outdated views and practices; develop strategic goals that embody its desired future, based on its mission and values; and measure performance based on these. It must cultivate innovation; finance the few initiatives that will make a difference; deploy resources where they will have the most impact; refine communication; provide continuous learning opportunities; initiate job rotation and expansion; create a marketing mind-set; listen to the customer; and recognize technology as a tool, not a driver. It must create dispersed, fluid leadership; facilitate leadership development and transition; focus on strengths rather than weaknesses; increase diversity; form strategic partnerships; and contribute to the community.

I was struggling to write this article about what leaders and organizations must do, today, to be viable and relevant 10 years from now. I told Rob Johnston, our president, that I thought the title would be "When the Roll Is Called in 2010." He left and shortly returned to my office with a Web site printout of a great old hymn I remember from my Methodist Sunday School days:

"When the Roll Is Called Up Yonder, I'll Be There." That wasn't exactly what I had in mind.

My concern is with how our actions today shape our legacy. Building a sustainable organization is one of a leader's primary responsibilities. When the challenges of today have been met, will your organization have the vigor to grow tomorrow? When the roll is called in 2010, will your organization be present?

Few social observers project that the years 2001–2010 will be easy ones for organizations in the public, private, and social sectors. Instead, *tenuous, turbulent,* and *tough* are the descriptors I hear when thought leaders evoke the future. But *inclusive, wide open,* and *promising* are part of the picture as well.

To meet the challenges and opportunities of the years to come requires hard work. My checklist—not for survival but for a successful journey to 2010—includes the following points:

✔ Revisiting the mission in 2003, 2006, and 2009, each time refining or amending it so that it reflects shifts in the environment and the changing needs of changing customers as part of a formal self-assessment process.

✔ Mobilizing the total organization around mission, until everyone including the newest secretary and the worker on the loading dock can tell you the mission of the enterprise—why it does what it does, its reason for being, its purpose.

✔ Developing no more than five powerful strategic goals that, together, are the board's vision of the desired future of the organization.

✔ Focusing on those few initiatives that will make a difference—not skimming the surface of an overstuffed list of priorities. Focus is key.

✔ Deploying people and allocating resources where they will have an impact, that is, only where they can further the mission and achieve the few powerful goals.

✔ Practicing Peter Drucker's "planned abandonment": jettisoning current policies, practices, and assumptions as soon as it becomes clear they will have little relevance in the future.

✔ Navigating the many streams of venture philanthropy, whether gearing up for the "ask" or as a philanthropist seeking to make an investment in changing the lives of people by partnering with a social sector organization.

✔ Expanding the definition of communication from saying something to being heard.

✔ Providing board members and the entire staff and workforce with carefully planned continuing learning opportunities designed to increase the capacity and unleash the creative energy of the people of the organization.

✔ Developing the leadership mind-set that embraces innovation as a life force, not as a technological improvement.

✔ Adopting Peter Drucker's definition: *Innovation is change that creates a new dimension of performance*.

✔ Structuring the finances of the organization—whether as seeker or funder in the social sector, business, or government—so that income streams are focused on the few great initiatives that will change lives, build community, and make a measurable difference.

✔ Transforming performance measurement into a management imperative that moves beyond the old forms and assumptions and toward creative and inclusive approaches to "measuring what we value and valuing what we measure."

✔ Scanning the environment and identifying major trends and implications for the organization in preparation for riding the wave of rapidly changing demographics.

✔ Building a mission-focused, values-based, demographics-driven organization.

✔ Planning for leadership transition in a thoughtful way. Leaving well and at the right moment is one of the greatest gifts a leader can give to the organization.

✔ Grooming successors—not a chosen one but a pool of gifted potential leaders. This is part of the leader's daily challenges.

✔ Making job rotation and job expansion into widespread organizational practices that are part of planning for the future.

✔ Dispersing the tasks of leadership across the organization until there are leaders at every level and dispersed leadership is the reality.

✔ Leading from the front, with leaders the embodiment of the mission and values in thinking, action, and communication.

✔ Recognizing technology not as driver but as tool. Changing the technology as needs change, not changing needs and style to match the tool. Shaping the future, not being shaped by it.

✔ Permeating every job, every plan with a marketing mindset. Marketing means being close to the customer and listening and responding to what the customer values.

✔ Building on strengths instead of dwelling on weaknesses until the organization has succeeded in, as Peter Drucker says, "making the strengths of our people effective and their weaknesses irrelevant."

✔ Throwing out the old hierarchy and building flexible, fluid, circular management systems with inclusive leader-ship language to match.

✔ Allocating funds for leadership development opportunities and resources for all the people of the enterprise.

✔ Developing the richly diverse organization so that board, management team, staff, employees, faculty, adminis-tration, and all communications materials reflect the diversity of the community, and we can respond with a resounding yes to the critical question: "When they look at us, can they find themselves?"

✔ Making every leader—every person who directs the work of others—accountable for building the richly diverse team, group, or organization.

✔ Keying individual performance appraisals to organizational performance.

✔ Governance is governance. Management is management. Sharply differentiating between the two by delineating clear roles, responsibilities, and accountabilities, resulting in a partnership of mutual trust and purpose. Building the partnership on open communication, adopting the philos-ophy of no surprises.

✔ Using a common leadership and management language within the organization and beyond with people and organizations in all three sectors around the world.

✔ Leading beyond the walls of the enterprise and building the organization's share of the healthy, cohesive community. Forming partnerships, alliances, and collaborations that spell synergy, success, and significance.

✔ This checklist for viability is only a beginning. Changing circumstances will require additions as new challenges arise, and deletions where needs have been met. New customers must be welcomed as we move beyond the old walls both physically and psychologically.

✔ Tomorrow may be tenuous for the leader and organization of the future, but the message is clear and powerful: Managing for mission, innovation, and diversity will sustain us and those we serve on the long journey to 2010.

Frances Hesselbein is editor in chief of *Leader to Leader,* chairman of the board of governors of the Drucker Foundation, and former chief executive of the Girl Scouts of the U.S.A.

2

Innovation

The New Route to New Wealth

Gary Hamel and Peter Skarzynski

Strategic life cycles are becoming shorter, and organizations that do not seek new opportunities will not succeed. By paying attention to demographics, changing technology, and consumer habits, organizations can sense needs that consumers have yet to articulate and develop new business models. Consciously creating an innovative environment involves recognizing that innovation and strategic insight don't result from corporate schedules, diversity of ideas exists across the organizational system, people need to feel safe in order to express divergent ideas, and there must be mechanisms to move from ideas to action.

W here does new wealth come from? Like a four-year-old's curiosity about how babies are born, it's a deceptively direct question that often disarms our capacity to answer. To be sure, we're ready with pat responses peppered with references to return on investment, return on net assets, and economic value added, but these measures tell us more about how revenues are rearranged than about how they're created anew. After all, we're not talking about market share sliced loose from a competitor or revenues boosted by an acquisitions binge—but truly new wealth: revenues from new customers buying products or services that yesterday they didn't know they needed and today can't live without.

Creating new wealth requires more than simply responding to market demand. Think about some of the path-breaking products of the past few decades. No car buyers walked into Chrysler dealerships in 1983 saying that what they really wanted was a van mounted on a car chassis with folding seats—and don't forget some cupholders. No customers told Sony the only thing wrong with its tape players was that you couldn't strap one on your head. Neither the BBC nor any of the Big Three U.S. TV networks saw a market for 24-hour news; it took a renegade named Turner operating out of Atlanta to wed three developments—the shoulder-held minicam, more affordable access to satellite transmission, and the fact that people no longer make it home in time for the six o'clock news—into the concept of a continuous news format. Innovations like the minivan, the Walkman, and CNN succeeded not because they responded to market need but because they created a need consumers had yet to sense themselves.

All of which attests to the fact that in the New Economy, the greatest rewards go to companies that create new business models—ideas that spark new sources of revenue based on changing technology, demographics, and consumer habits. By definition, new business models destroy old ones, which is why creating new wealth is a threat to every traditional, unimaginative business. Never before have strategy life cycles been shorter and has market leadership counted for less. Call it the First Law of the Innovation Economy: Companies that are not constantly pursuing innovation will soon be overwhelmed by it. Strategy innovation is the only way to deal with discontinuous—and disruptive— change.

The Innovation Imperative

Some companies seem to understand the innovation imperative instinctively. Consider Charles Schwab's daring plunge into the online unknown: When the bricks-and-mortar broker took the view that online trading was inevitable, it faced a choice between leading the brokerage industry to the future or being a victim of some dot-com start-up that got there first. Thus, on the fateful day in 1995 when a technology team within Schwab presented a demo of what the Web could do, senior managers almost instantly recognized how the Internet could make life better for Schwab customers. Schwab invested in the Web even before it realized it would face aggressive price-based competition from other Web brokers. By committing to the goal—and pursuing it through a series of low-risk experiments—Schwab was able to establish a dominant position in the online trading world.

Today, Schwab controls some 30 percent of all the stock trading that takes place on the Web. Even more impressive, Schwab's market capitalization—$3.5 billion in 1995, less than half that of Merrill Lynch—has now pulled even with Merrill's, which instead of engaging the Internet, pursued until recently a policy of digital denial.

You're Never Too Old to Innovate

Schwab is not an upstart. And innovation isn't the special preserve of Internet upstarts or the denizens of the dot-com motels of Silicon Valley. In fact, innovation can happen at any company, regardless of its line of business, age, or location.

Can a century-old company learn to innovate like an industry ingenue? The answer is yes—provided the company is willing to examine its orthodoxies, abandon its strategy-by-habit ways, and engage its employees broadly and deeply in the effort to envision the new markets and new opportunities that promise new wealth.

Consider the experience of PECO Energy Corporation—the old Philadelphia Electric Company. Founded in 1881, PECO had operated for its entire existence within the public utility paradigm, with a regulatory strategy that brought it significant success. In June 1997, however, the company was looking to transform its regulatory strategy to fit the dawning deregulated environment.

Working to examine its hidden assumptions, PECO uncovered a core competency in operating large, mission-critical infrastructure—a competency honed in time of crisis a decade earlier when PECO grappled with bringing its own Peach Bottom nuclear plant into federal compliance. PECO emerged from the Peach Bottom process with a proven ability to bring "problem plants" to high-capacity performance with low operating costs.

As a result, where other companies saw liabilities, PECO saw opportunity. PECO would follow its competency into places other companies feared to tread—taking on responsibility for running environmentally risky nuclear plants in a safe, efficient manner. PECO has now bought three U.S. nuclear plants that had been for sale for years—including a reactor at Pennsylvania's notorious Three Mile Island, obtained for $23 million—a substantial discount from its $640 million book value.

The problem-plant strategy proved just one element of a broader innovation agenda. PECO teams looked beyond their traditional market to tomorrow's opportunities. A prime example: PECO conceived of the wire that delivers electricity into each home as a pipeline permitting a far wider carrying capacity.

The company built on its core competency in power delivery networks to launch a new communications platform. Exelon, a subsidiary of PECO Energy, has strung 27,000 miles of high-speed telecommunications line atop electrical transmission poles—and signed up over 100,000 phone customers in its first year in operation. PECO now looks to combine the installation of electric, gas, telephone, and cable to provide a single-source installation service for its customers.

Three Signs

What's standing in the way of companies that fail to innovate? In many cases, it is the tried-and-true recipe that brought them past success.

It's understandable. Businesses with a winning formula are logically reluctant to change horses in midstream. Over time, however, every business model and every strategy goes stale—and in our fast-forward economy, strategies reach their "sell-by" date faster than ever. Indeed, the life cycle of successful business strategies has been rapidly declining in a period of high competition and innovation. In the Industrial Age, a successful business strategy for steel manufacture or durable goods might power a company for a generation or more; today, Moore's Law (which states that computing power and speed double every 18 months) is setting the terms for strategy life cycles that are measured in months, not years.

How can a company tell if its present profits come from spending down past success? Here are three new realities to consider:

• *The inevitability of commoditization.* Every new product or service will become a commodity in time. Not many years ago, cell phones cost upwards of $100; today, companies will give you one to sell you their service. Likewise, phone service itself is now a commodity: Traditional telecoms—local as well as long-distance—are engaged in a race to the bottom to see who can sell access to a dial tone for how little. Meanwhile, Internet upstarts are considering giving away long-distance calls to lure people to their site, while deriving their revenue from advertising and other sources.

• *The impossibility of forecasting future trends.* Most forecasts are worthless exercises in spreadsheet manipulation—and not just because small adjustments in key variables create wildly different projections over time. The larger problem is that traditional forecasting projects past assumptions forward, providing a sense of false comfort to established companies wedded to existing business models. It's like auto industry forecasters painting a reassuring picture of steadily rising minivan and family sedan sales—the year before Ford rolled out something it called the Sports Utility Vehicle. Whatever industry you're in, you can't drive change looking in the rear view mirror.

• *The futility of waiting for inspiration.* If it's a given that great companies are built on a brilliant idea, the next question is where the next great idea will come from. Don't be fooled by the rosy glow of growth: Companies living off a single great insight are the corporate equivalent of dead stars—in spite of their sparkle, they're cold at the core. Like grandma's favorite "Five and Dime" store in the age of category-killers and cyber-shopping info-bots: Stand pat with your original business model, and burnout is only a matter of time.

Creating an Innovation Engine

If companies can't depend on the lightning bolt of sudden inspiration or serendipitous discovery, then what? An innovative environment can be consciously created—if a company is willing to abandon old rules, shed old habits, and upend cherished conventions. The key is recognizing that past achievement militates against future adaptability by creating well-worn ways of doing things that cause a company to undervalue or ignore rule-breaking insights. Yesterday's laserlike focus becomes today's set of blinders, narrowing an enterprise's field of vision from what is truly new to what it already knows. Glimmers of great ideas are evident in most organizations; the problem is that in direct proportion to the degree those great ideas are different, the "immune system" of most organizations attacks those ideas as foreign organisms, threatening the host.

Part of the challenge is demystifying innovation by breaking it down to its constituent parts. Here are three ways to begin the process of awakening innovation in your company:

• *Recognize that innovation doesn't follow a schedule.* Most companies are so bounded by existing orthodoxies and obsolete business models that they think they can schedule strategic insight the way you record a reminder in your day-planner. But the truly innovative bursts of insight that trigger new ideas don't obey the corporate planning calendar.

Consider that the idea for Nokia's wildly successful rainbow-hued cell phones emerged not from a daylong strategy session in the corner office but from an afternoon at California's Venice Beach, as company execs watched sun-drenched skaters slash down the boardwalk, sporting color-coordinated shades, Rollerblades, and bathing suits. The realization: Mobile phones are as much fashion accessory as communications tool, an inspiration that's pushed Nokia to the cutting edge of cells.

• *Shatter the "strategy monopoly."* In any company, a hierarchy of organization dominates a hierarchy of ideas. The antidote: To encourage innovation, unlock ideas from across the company. Bring together a cross-section of employees at all levels to share the new perspectives that may just contain the kernel of a bold new idea. Realize that every company promotes success as defined by today's reigning strategy; the question is how to promote new ideas that may have nothing to do with that strategy—or may even cut against it.

That's how Virgin Enterprises operates under the lead of Richard Branson. Every employee has Branson's phone number and can pitch new project ideas directly to the top. That's how a Virgin Airlines flight attendant turned her difficulties in planning her own wedding into a new venture: the wedding planning boutique Virgin Bride.

• *Institutionalize innovation by building a safe place for people to think new thoughts.* In some companies, new ideas are in short supply—stifled by a corporate climate that cuts off intellectual oxygen, discourages change, and demands conformity. At other companies, ideas abound—and the challenge takes a different shape: Creating the conceptual conveyor belt that moves from ideas to action.

From Ideas to Action

Can a company really institutionalize innovation? Witness the effort of Royal Dutch/Shell, the Anglo-Dutch oil giant. With $138 billion in revenues, 102,000 employees, and nearly a century-old tradition, Shell is the epitome of a lumbering industrial behemoth—the last place you'd expect to find entrepreneurial zeal. Within Shell's Balkanized organization—which one employee compared to a maze of 100-foot-high brick walls—access to capital is tightly controlled, investment hurdles are daunting, and radical ideas move slowly, if at all. Shell's globe-trotting managers are famously disciplined, diligent, and methodical. In cataloguing their character and capabilities, "wild-eyed dreamers" is not a term that comes to mind.

Enter Shell's GameChanger initiative, begun in 1996. As an incentive to innovate, a group of Shell employees were given the authority to allocate $20 million to rule-breaking, game-changing ideas submitted by their peers. Proposals would be accepted from anywhere within the company—no need to squeeze radical new ideas through the keyhole of existing programs and priorities.

Shell's GameChanger team embarked on an Action Lab, an intensive five-day experience designed to dramatically accelerate the translation of "gamechanging" ideas into practical venture plans for the launch of new businesses—plans of the kind that would pass muster with venture capitalists in Silicon Valley. The goal was for each team to present its story to a "venture board"—a panel of senior Shell executives and representatives from Shell Technology Ventures Inc., a unit whose job is to fund late-stage technology commercialization. The venture board was empowered by GameChanger to "sponsor" winning concepts and fund the next round of business development. In the end, four teams out of the original twelve received six-month funding to put them on a path toward full-fledged business plans.

For Shell, GameChanger was the beginning of an attempt to institutionalize innovation. Today, any employee with a promising idea is invited to give a 10-minute pitch to the panel, followed by a 15-minute Q&A session. Ideas that get a green light often receive funding—on average, $100,000, but sometimes as much as

$600,000—within eight or ten days. Ideas that don't pass muster enter a database accessible to anyone within Shell, a kind of innovation stockpot that helps entrepreneurial employees shape their own ideas or bring new insight to existing ones. To date, several of GameChanger's ventures have found homes in a Shell operating unit or in one of the company's various growth initiatives. Still others have been carried forward as R&D projects, while the remainder have been wound down and written off as interesting but unproductive experiments.

GameChanger is producing measurable results: Of Shell's five largest growth initiatives for 1999, four had their genesis in the GameChanger—including one exploring an entirely new business focused on renewable geothermal energy sources. Fully 30 percent of Shell's exploration and production R&D budget is now devoted to ventures that are GameChanger graduates.

As the Shell case suggests, it is possible to create an internal constituency for change—inspiring a new breed of "innovation activist" to find an ear and an outlet for creative new concepts within a company. Compared to innovation-unfriendly organizations that leave their iconoclasts no option but to take their bright ideas elsewhere, Shell's experience proves that established companies can create a hospitable climate for change.

Hammer Time

What can innovation-minded executives do to create such a culture in their company? Here are three ways to kick-start the innovation process:

• *Start new conversations*. New ideas don't obey an organizational chart. Companies that want to get serious about innovation need to break the "strategy monopoly" that closes off the executive suite from new ideas percolating in other corners of the company. Innovation-minded companies spark new conversations by bringing together executives with employees of all ranks to question corporate orthodoxies and search for new ways to do business.

• *Seek new perspectives*. If you want your company to do a better job of envisioning the future, ask the people who will get to the future first: your youngest employees. If you want to know how consumers act, don't observe them in focus-group captivity—join the Nokia execs for a day at the beach. Want a new vision? Try a new vantage point—and watch a world of opportunity open up.

• *Spark new passions*. Innovation comes from the heart as well as the head. Companies that aren't afraid to innovate engage employee energies in a new and profoundly different way. When people are part of a cause and not just a cog in the wheel, their IQ—innovation quotient—skyrockets.

And above all, recognize that in today's economy, capital is plentiful; good ideas are scarce. Companies that look to incremental change to generate additional revenue will tend toward subsistence at best—eclipsed by companies that create an environment of innovation, spawning the new ideas that generate new wealth. That's why an ambitious enterprise must replicate within itself the basic DNA of innovation: a culture of continuous experimentation embedded broadly and deeply throughout a company.

All of which brings us to the final characteristic of the true innovator: *courage*—the guts to realize it's time to take a hammer to your own business model, before someone else does it for you.

Gary Hamel is founder and chairman of Strategos, a consulting firm focused on strategy innovation, and is visiting professor of strategic and international management at the London Business School. A frequent contributor to *Harvard Business Review*, *Fortune*, and the *Wall Street Journal*, Hamel is coauthor of the best-selling *Competing for the Future* and author of *Leading the Revolution*.

Peter Skarzynski is CEO and a founding partner of Strategos. His work on strategy, innovation, and enterprise systems has spanned a number of industries, including consumer products, energy, telecommunications, and high technology. He has written for *Chief Executive*, *Management Review*, and the *San Jose Mercury News*. Previously he was vice president of consumer products at Gemini Consulting.

3

The Spice of Life

An Interview with Stephen Jay Gould

*In this interview, Stephen Jay Gould discusses the limited
basis for applying concepts of natural evolution to cultural
change in social systems. In such systems, acquired characteristics can be inherited, and the speed of change is much
greater than it is in natural selection. However, a few comparisons can be made. Biology and human systems are
composed of many interacting components in which small
changes in one can have cascading effects throughout. With
the added effect of randomness, prediction becomes very
difficult, and statistics may not reflect reality. In biology,
separation is forever, whereas different human systems can
combine to create something new. Organizations must be
sensitive to rapid shifts in the environment and be flexible
enough to adapt to changing conditions.*

F ew scientists have reached a wider audience than Stephen
Jay Gould. Passionate intellectual, best-selling author, and
devoted baseball fan, Gould finds inspiration far beyond his life-
long study of paleontology. In his acclaimed *Full House*, for instance, he combines evolutionary science, statistics, and
professional sports to explain the nature of randomness, diversity, and variation in all living systems—themes that have
struck a chord with many organizational thinkers. He spoke
with Paul Cohen on what biology has to do with management.

Paul Cohen: In recent years, biology has had a huge influence on organizational theory. The phrase "complex adaptive systems" may occur as often in business journals as in scientific ones. Do these principles legitimately apply to management?

Stephen Jay Gould: Often when these kinds of analogical comparisons are made it's far-fetched or merely metaphorical. This is one of these cases where it may not be. Businesses are natural complex systems, and species are complex systems, so there ought to be some similarities. It is not a question of misapplying biological truths to human systems; it is a case of looking at principles which apply to both biology and human systems. Both are composed of large numbers of interacting components in which small changes in one can have cascading implications throughout.

On the other hand, the attempt to apply natural selection theory—the adaptation of a species to changing local environments—to the business world is wrong in principle. The mechanics of change in human cultural institutions are quite different from those in nature. For one thing, the inheritance of human institutions is Lamarckian—that is, it is an application of the theory (which is incorrect in nature) that acquired characteristics can be passed on to the next generation. But fortunately that happens all the time in human culture. It is called learning. So the analogy to natural evolution doesn't work. But complexity theory actually has a potential common basis.

PC: What do you think we can learn from complexity theory?

SJG: I think it can help us to understand why prediction is so difficult. For one thing, management is not a science like physics or astronomy where you have complete predictability. I can tell you to the minute when the next eclipse is going to occur, because it's a simple system with limited interactions. I can't tell you where human evolution is going. Also, the mathematical analysis of complex systems—systems composed of multiple, independent parts—shows that a small perturbation can produce profound effects, because of the way it cascades through the non-linear interactions of the system. If you then add a little bit of randomness you get profound and unpredictable effects.

It's just natural—not only in business, but in any human endeavor—to think that we can figure out how we want a system to change, study the laws of change, and do our best to make it happen. But often you don't know what the optimal or better adapted system might be. Sometimes allowing a degree of randomness to operate in systems is the best strategy—especially if you don't know where things ought to be going. Just let the system float in a Darwinian world; it will probably find its best locally adaptive form. Those will be the survivors.

PC: That does not sound like a clearly defined strategy for change.

SJG: To operate under Darwinian principles—to put out a lot of variation and see where it goes—sounds brutal and inefficient, and it is. In fact, Darwin himself recognized how inefficient the system of natural selection is. In a famous letter he wrote to his friend Joseph Hooker in the 1840s, Darwin said, "What a work a Devil's chaplain would make of the miserable, low blundering and inefficient ways of nature."

Natural selection is not a very efficient system because it works by elimination. You get to goodness by eliminating the bad. Why don't you just go to good? The problem is, you don't know what good is. You have to let a system operate and find itself. That kind of modeling is counterintuitive to the way in which humans generally try to run their institutions. It may not always work—but it's had some success in medicine, for example. If you don't know what drug combination is going to work, why not just try a lot—not on people, obviously.

PC: We know that evolution is not a matter of continuous, gradual improvement but one of fits and starts or "punctuated equilibrium." Similar patterns hold for entire industries through history. What does that suggest about how to manage change?

SJG: The world is too complex to be in continuous flux in all its parts. If you have continuous flux in every part of a system, how are you ever going to get integrated, complex systems? Lester Thurow, in his book *The Future of Capitalism*, identifies punctuated equilibrium as one of the three or four notions in the sciences that work well to describe the history of economic change. His message is that, at the very least, we have to be sensitive to rapid shifts in the business and political environment.

PC: You write that evolution is "a full house of variation within a whole system" rather than a clear march of progress toward a higher life form . . .

SJG: Yes, bacteria still dominate the world, as they always will.

PC: But does the role of variation and diversity have implications for those who manage human systems?

SJG: I can only tell you, as a personal example, that I live in SoHo in New York, and I love that there's the corner Korean grocery that's open 24 hours. It is one of many elements of a very rich environment. I realize that there are all sorts of pressures to standardization. But I think of another principle of evolution: diversity and regionalism. If you have a species that lives over a wide area, it's going to diversify into regional groups called subspecies. I value that in human society, and I hope we don't go to a model of universal maximal efficiency and only one way to do everything. In fact, ultimately that doesn't work, because of punctuated equilibrium and the nature of environmental change. If you do put your eggs in one basket, that basket's going to eventually collapse. And diversity gives you resiliency against catastrophe.

PC: You have shown how misleading it can be to rely on statistical averages for a true picture of reality. Can you explain why that is and what leaders should use as a more meaningful indicator of performance?

SJG: I'm not saying that the trend of either an average or an extreme value is never an appropriate measure. It might be, for certain kinds of questions. It's just that we do have a tendency, and a very erroneous one, to look at entire systems, which are highly variable, and then to abstract that variation in a single number which interests us. Then we use the trend of that single number to characterize the whole system. We can just make ridiculous errors by doing that. Yes, if you've got a few Bill Gateses in a country, some happy politician will say "the mean income has risen substantially." But when you look at the mode—that is, the most commonly occurring value—you may find that most people's income has actually fallen. If you don't look at the whole variation within a system, you'll get a very misleading view of the nature of things.

Often you can just plot the full range through time rather than worry about what is happening at a single moment, as expressed by an average or an extreme.

PC: What are the sources of improvement, or continued change and adaptability, in a healthy system?

SJG: With Darwinian theory, as we discussed, there's no notion of general advance. There is adaptation to a changing environment. Darwinian theory is about constant local improvement, and since environments are always changing, especially given technological progress, there always has to be flexibility for adaptation—more so in human cultural systems. No matter how well you're doing something, your environment may change. A travel agent offering the friendliest service in the business finds the next month that everybody's buying their tickets online. One answer is to remember that natural selection is about local adjustment, not about cosmic betterment.

PC: Speaking of cosmic issues, you make the case in *Full House* that the disappearance of .400 hitting in baseball actually reflects an improvement in the game. In essence, everyone is getting better, so there is simply less room for an individual to tower above the rest. How do we manage in a context where all competitors are strong and the potential for great improvement is small?

SJG: In human technological history, we may reach that point in certain forms of human invention. When, for instance, you reach the limit in speed of communication, which, of course, is instantaneity, you're not going to get any faster. But I think in most of human technology, we're nowhere near those kinds of limits. The issue more often applies to the human body because we can get ourselves to the extreme of what a body can conceivably do. I suppose there are situations in the world of business where we're approaching the limit of what, in principle, a system could do. In those cases, I would think, you play to your strength and look for other areas of improvement.

PC: Does the fact that in 1998 both Mark McGwire and Sammy Sosa crushed a 37-year-old record and in 1999 came close to matching those records change your view that modern players are nearing the limits of what is possible?

SJG: I wouldn't look at it that way. McGwire in 1998 was a man of destiny. You have to remember, he hit 49 in his rookie year. He's got great gifts of body, and that obsessiveness in training. He hit 58 the year before and missed two or three weeks. I've been saying for years, if he ever plays a full season he's definitely going to break the record. Sosa is the one who somewhat mystifies me. He is a wonderful player, but I don't know where his recent performance comes from—1998 was a replay of Maris and Mantle with reverse results. Mantle was the man of destiny in 1961. He didn't quite make it. Maris had never hit more than 39, came out of nowhere. But McGwire is the Ruth of this generation, and every once in a while someone's going to come along and do it.

PC: You have said that we've developed a cult of innovation in which we honor the new over the enduring. And yet innovation is by definition the way forward. Can one assess the quality of an idea in order to avoid what others have called an infatuation with mindless change?

SJG: Indeed, one can. Of course, I'm a paleontologist so I revere the past in ways that not everyone does. If you consider the aesthetic and the ethical dimension, then you're not going to always worship innovation. Sometimes we do things in ways that may not be maximally efficient because they have human value.

What amuses me is how often people will go for complex technologies that automate things—which in general I'm in favor of—at the expense of simplicity. For example, old-fashioned photographic slide technology works pretty well because it's not complicated. A human being presses a button and you get the slide you want. It very rarely fails and if it does you have a person right there to fix it.

Now you've got portable computers. Someday they'll work flawlessly, and then I'll switch to them. But for the moment, I've never seen one that works reliably. And their results, even when they do work, aren't much better than a set of conventional slides. That's a case where I think you really don't need it.

PC: As science and technology play an increasing role in society, do you see a global leadership role for scientists? Should they be more involved in articulating a vision for the future?

SJG: I think so, and I think that we do insofar as we can and that people listen. I don't think scientists have any superior political sense, nor can we predict the future any better than any pundit in politics or history or sociology. But we do have technical knowledge that's enormously important—the understanding of how all these devices work. I don't think it gives us any moral compass; but since science can be politicized, we want scientists to be speaking out on these issues.

PC: The human genome project makes it likely that, in a generation or two, humans will be able to plan their own genetic development. Again, at the risk of getting cosmic, will that change our view of our place in the universe?

SJG: That's a little broad. It certainly changes a lot of things about human culture. The scope of the change will depend first on how much regulation we impose upon it, and I think we'll impose a lot. Second, of course, most of the traits we really want are not coded in the genes. You will be able to choose blue eyes versus brown eyes; that is simple. And you will be able to select for sex, which raises serious ethical concerns. But you're not going to be able to choose intelligence—I don't doubt there are lots of genes that influence intelligence—but there isn't a "smart gene." With such a complex interaction of thousands of genes with environmental factors, there is not going to be a simple menu for the things we really care about.

PC: Finally, given all the analogies and imposed models that you see—what actual lessons does natural evolution offer for society and organizations?

SJG: I think rather limited ones. And that's an important point. There are meaningful analogies, we've been talking about some of them, but the main error people make is to take a well-articulated and well-confirmed mechanism of Darwinian change, that is, natural selection, and think it ought to describe cultural change in humans as well. It really doesn't in principle. Those are the errors of 19th-century social Darwinism.

The entire mechanics of change is so different in cultural versus natural systems. In cultural systems change is Lamarckian—acquired characteristics can be inherited. Whatever we learn or invent in one generation we teach directly to the next generation. That gives cultural change a powerful driving force.

That's why the speed of cultural change works at orders of magnitude greater than anything possible with natural selection. And why natural selection has almost become irrelevant in human evolution. There's been no biological change in humans in 40,000 or 50,000 years. Everything we call culture and civilization we've built with the same body and brain.

The other major difference is that in natural biological evolution once a lineage becomes separate, it's separate forever. It interacts with others ecologically but it can't join with them to create something new. But in human culture you do that all the time. A traveler to a distant land sees a wheel, goes back home, and changes his culture forever—so you have constant cross-penetration. Which again makes things unpredictable and wildly variable and fast moving.

I think the only thing that evolutionary theory suggests that's analogical is that genetic variability is a good thing, so therefore flexibility, different strategies, ability to change, variation, ability to consider lots of alternatives are also good—the only constancy is change, and you need flexibility for adaptation. Species that are very rigidly committed to one way of life don't last very long.

Stephen Jay Gould is Alexander Agassiz Professor of Zoology and professor of geology at Harvard University and is curator for invertebrate paleontology at the university's Museum of Comparative Zoology. He also serves as the Vincent Astor Visiting Professor of Biology at New York University and is author of more than 16 books, including *Full House* and *Questioning the Millennium*.

4

Gene Politics and the Natural Selection of Leaders

Nigel Nicholson

We have created a complex technological world, but we have inherited the genetic traits of clan-dwelling hunter-gatherers. In our society, the two routes to the top are social dominance (power) and achievement. We tend to admire leaders who possess both. Some ineffectual leaders lack motivation and the abilities that need to accompany it, and some are not good at managing people. We need leaders who are orchestrators, collaborators, and facilitators. Dominance and achievement must be coupled with integration, empowerment, and community building. Selection must be expanded to value creators, challengers, team builders, and nurturing coaches, in addition to fighters and chieftans. The best balance may be achieved through shared leadership.

Leaders have two main functions in the life of a community. One is to help the organization define and achieve its purposes—this is the leader's role in formulating strategy, vision, and challenge. The other is to embody the spirit of the community and help hold it together. In the healthy community these go hand in hand.

But look around the business world and what do you see? Flashy egomaniacs running their people ragged while neglecting their welfare. Chronic loners sequestered behind oak-paneled doors to formulate arcane strategy. Detail-obsessed bosses scarcely daring to venture into the outside world and spending all their time trying to do everyone else's job. Yes, we have some gifted leaders, but they are rare.

It's not surprising then that there is so much focus on what it takes to be a strong leader, but the literature of leadership is strangely disempowering—asking us to do the difficult today and the impossible tomorrow. Our bookshop shelves are groaning with volumes plying us with yet more lists of desirable attributes, heroic and cautionary tales, and recipes for success. The traditional academic literature contained numerous sensible observations about how you needed different leadership styles for different situations but without telling you how to change either style or situation. Today, transformational leadership and emotional intelligence are in vogue. This literature hectors leaders to stay tuned in and switched on to human feelings and motives—it's no longer enough to be a technical visionary, a fearless negotiator, or an accomplished mentor.

What all of these volumes fail to point out is obvious to people who work in the real world—that is, many of us simply don't have what it takes be a leader, at least as the role is played in today's organizations. Does that mean we should all give up and go home? No, but it does suggest that we should seriously question what we expect of our leaders and how the nature of our organizations means we get the leaders we deserve, more or less. How does the local organizational environment bias our choice of leaders? Are the models of leadership we get as a result too narrow? How do these models fit the kinds of instincts, capacities, and social predilections most of us bring to our work?

The New Discipline
of Evolutionary Psychology

To address such questions it is useful to turn to the emerging discipline of evolutionary psychology. It presents a new view of the world and our place within it that is not always comforting. The message is challenging not just for business, but every area of our lives. The discipline also rewrites many of the accepted orthodoxies of social science thinking, offering nothing less than a unifying framework of ideas for all our fields of social inquiry.

The vision posed by evolutionary psychology is so compelling because it is science based. Its radical insight was originally Charles Darwin's, now updated with the latest advances in a whole range of disciplines: paleontology, neuroscience, archaeology, anthropology, biology, and ethology. Through the neo-Darwinian lens social scientists—economists, lawyers, psychologists, and sociologists—are finding common cause with the natural scientists. The core insight is simple but far-reaching. It is that we inhabit a world crammed with our own creations—technical marvels and complex social arrangements—with the unreconstructed minds of Stone Age men and women. The swelling body of evidence developed by a new generation of writers, thinkers, and scientists—people such as biologist Richard Dawkins, psychiatrist Randolph Nesse, and economist Robert Frank—supports three principles:

- The human mind is not a blank slate to be written on by experience but an organ stacked with genetically encoded routines, biases, and goals that aid our survival and reproduction.

- Evolution designed this mind to fit us, as it designed our bodies, for a lifestyle that predominated for the

4 million years or so of our evolution—the life of clan-dwelling hunter-gatherers.

- There has been no significant evolution in our psychology or physiology in the few thousand years since we abandoned this lifestyle. There has been insufficient time and no consistent selective pressure to move our design in any single significant new direction.

This account has some tough implications. One is that we cannot keep pace with our own inventions and, as a result, we get into serious misfits with the situations we create. Another is that there are limits to what we can change about ourselves. In business it suggests we had better start managing *with* rather than *against* the grain of human nature.

What does this have to do with leadership? Plenty. First, some people are more fit to be leaders than others, while some are born with other gifts. Second, the organizations that we have created—much like the modern lifestyles we have created—in many cases may be totally out of synch with how our brains are wired for leadership.

The Born Leader

Maybe the biggest disconnect between the leadership literature and what people experience every day in organizations is the issue of who can and should be a leader. Anyone with their eyes open in the office or factory can see that there are three broad bands of people around them. The first are people with confidence, drive, and ability who tend to find their way into positions of influence wherever they find themselves. A second group—the antithesis of the first—are people who may have other strengths but lack these qualities and will never be anyone's conscious choice for leadership. In between is a third mixed group of people with some potential who might make it into leadership roles if the conditions are just right for them.

The big lie sold to us by much of the management literature is the myth that any man or woman can be turned into a leader, given the right developmental intervention. The truth is that people are hardwired to be different from one another in the attributes that make people choose to be, or make them chosen to be, leaders. The new science of behavior genetics is steadily accumulating evidence about how much of individual character, style, and competence is inborn. As every parent with more than one child knows, each is born different and stays different. Childhood experience and radical change in adulthood can do some reworking to our traits, but mostly by the time we are in our early 20s the dials of our character have been set and will change little. Some of those differences directly bear upon fitness for leadership. The most important of these is the motive to lead, plus the ability and constitution to support this drive.

In modern organizations there are generally two ways to the top. One is personal, through *social dominance*. These are people who are likely to be in charge of every situation they are in, desiring power over and responsibility for other people. They often have developed the social and political skills to support this drive. The other route to the top is by *achievement*—the competitive strivers who want to attain status through visible success and expertise in some field of their choice. These two drives, dominance and status, are quite different, but both lead to the top. The first gives you power over people. The second gives you reputation and eminence.

The leaders we tend to admire are those who possess both drives, plus matching abilities: they are ambitious and accomplished; at the same time they are respected for their influence. But we also see unbalanced types: the leaders who seem not really to like people—leaders who drove their way to the top by being the best at something other than managing human beings. Their counterparts are individuals who exhibit only raw social power and the desire to be dominant. And then, occasionally, there are the weak, ineffectual, stressed-out, and chaotic leaders who have neither the critical motives nor the abilities that need to accompany them.

And why do we get ill-suited leaders? They come to positions of power through the selective biases of their organizational cultures.

The Leadership
Our Organizations Demand

Natural selection operates by favoring traits that assist survival and reproduction, and eliminating those that don't. The logic of selection operates in every aspect of our daily lives—in how we gravitate toward situations that fit us and try to avoid areas where we feel uncomfortable. In our work lives, there are two sides to this selection. On one side is the organization. Think of an organization in its structure and culture as a network of selective biases. Some big corporations have split personalities in this respect—functions or divisions can have quite different cultures, criteria, and methods of selecting and managing people.

On the other side of the equation are the individuals on which environments practice their selection. This operates not just at the level of who joins but also in placement and promotion—who gets put in key slots and who gets passed over. Sometimes the selection process operates with a naked and obvious power. Sometimes it is subtle and insidious. Moreover, it is a two-way street. People are not just chosen; they get to choose too. People can refuse positions, turn down promotions, and seek opportunities elsewhere. The result is a sorting out that elevates some people to leadership positions and passes over others. This happens in different ways across the business world.

The leadership models that this assortment yields are often dysfunctional. One of the most common examples of today's hypercompetitive business environment is the firm that demands street-fighter dominance. In the political scramble for market power, nice guys and gals not only get passed over, they walk away from the opportunities that get presented to them. Firms that get rich on slash-and-burn management also die by the sword. The crash of Sunbeam and its leader Al "Chainsaw" Dunlap, as documented by John Byrne in *Chainsaw*, provides a telling parable on this theme.

The solution is not easy—nothing less than a culture change that restores some sense of community will do. An ideal fit with human nature is the communitarian model of organization and leadership that is found in hunter-gatherer clans. Anthropological observation and historical reconstruction show that within their fluid hierarchies leadership occurred on multiple dimensions. Leader roles served the essential tasks of the clan, and the community respected and honored the authority of its superior men and women. Locked into these communities was the full range of human types—birth and death were the near-exclusive entry and exit routes. Contact with strangers and external communities in a sparsely populated world would have been rare.

These conditions are long gone. Now we live in a world in which there is much contact among different organizational clans and individuals move freely between them. Interestingly, this leads to a sort of cloning, not diversity, and the risk of con-formist rigidity. Like attracts like, especially in businesses with refined technical missions, and the people who rise to the top are often the most ambitious chief technicians. They have a brilliant understanding of their businesses and strong power needs but often are desperately poor with people. I recently worked with a European pharmaceuticals company that had de-veloped this pathology. The chief—a senior scientist—took the opportunity of a top management event to publicly humiliate some of his senior colleagues by pointing the finger at their busi-ness failings, instead of supplying the rallying cry they craved. To humanize such businesses requires a loosening of the selec-tion forces that create conformity, but the paradox is that their cloning is often the source of their power in the market.

Another type of business leadership model is the self-made leader. This is the man or woman who would have difficulty sur-viving in any conventional business, whose drives and gifts pre-clude contentment as number two and certainly not in any lower position in the hierarchy. Such individuals use their talent to build businesses around their unique identities. The firms they create often die as they grow, because the unemployable leader also turns out to be a lousy employer, unable to shepherd people through the transition from entrepreneurial to managed firm. But some do. Many major corporations bear the indelible stamp of the identity of their founder—like Dell in the United States, Virgin in the United Kingdom, and Ikea in Sweden. The question then becomes whether the firm can survive the leader's eventual de-parture. Many family firms cannot make it through intergenera-tional succession because boss Junior lacks the qualities of boss Senior, which even the best finishing schools and most elaborate grooming for power cannot instill.

A final type we should not forget is the classic bureaucracy, a form that continues to operate with great success around the world. As the sociologist Max Weber pointed out, the beauty of bureaucracy is that it is relatively immune to bad (and good) leadership, so long as standard operating procedures make all the decisions. But of course systems and rules can't cover all the bases, and leadership creeps in through the side entrance. People who like to work in bureaucracies—almost itself a self-disqualifying quality for inspired leadership—get transported to positions of limited power by seniority or by virtue of their qualifications. This turns out to be wild-card leadership. Where selection is not on the basis of personal qualities you never know quite what you're going to get. But bureaucracies are designed to cope with this through fail-safes and power limitations. Leadership is often safely predictable, but there is precious little magic.

One side effect of the selective logic that predominates in much of the business world is that it is hard for women to rise to power. They often find the hypercompetitive model uncongenial, and the cloning model of technical businesses puts them at a disadvantage. The result is that many women are taking another route—dropping out of male-dominated competitive hierarchies to build businesses around their identities and distinctive visions: as Mary Kay Ash did in the United States and Anita Roddick did in the United Kingdom with The Body Shop. Women also often do better in the bureaucratic model, so long as the escalators of power have little or no selective bias.

Better Leaders—Make or Buy?

To get better leaders, we need better organizations—organizations that can work with human nature rather than against it, conforming more closely to the communitarian model for which our hunter-gatherer brains are best adapted. There is a chicken-and-egg problem here, however. Culture change is an essential element of the equation, which we know to be notoriously difficult and to require inspired leadership. Yet we can begin to resolve the problem by choosing better leaders while embarking on change, even as we select those who can best lead change. This means evaluating and selecting individuals on a broader spectrum than most promotion systems pay attention to. The inspired creator, the challenger of orthodoxy, the team builder, the nurturing coach, and other varieties need to be accorded more respect and responsibility. Once cultures start to become more communitarian then the emergence of leaders through natural selection can become more trusted. Groups often are rather good at spotting which of their members as leaders would best fulfill the key tasks required of them by the community: defining purpose and fostering integration.

As to leader development, we should abandon the fiction that we can shape a person's character. Leadership style can be moderated but not transformed. The best we can do is instill some basic rules and intelligence about the leadership process and train people to practice the key behaviors and habits that we know to be associated with effective leadership. This agenda can go quite far toward helping those people who have some potential but who aren't naturally gifted leaders. They can be trained in the skills of communicating, goal setting, and motivating, for example. In many firms with sound business processes and systems that aren't undergoing fundamental change or that don't have special leadership needs, this may be enough.

A New Type of Leader for a New Age?

The vision being promoted of the New Economy conjures images of virtual corporations and networked alliances, led by a new breed of leaders who are less traditional bosses than they are orchestrators, collaborators, and facilitators. Among their ranks will be many women, and those men who excel in the arts of communication, teamworking, and innovation.

There is both truth and falsehood to this vision. The falsehood is to imagine that we are entering a totally transformed world in which the rules of business will be rewritten. The reality is that we cannot eat virtual bread or work at virtual machines. We inhabit—and will continue to inhabit—a world in which things need to be made and delivered on schedule, often in large quantities and to exact specifications. Every dot-com rests on a network of businesses with traditional elements of function and design, and within these the work of managers and leaders is going to remain largely unchanged. Moreover, even dot-coms need to be well managed, and the same qualities that have always propelled the motivated leader to the top will be needed by these firms as they grow into hierarchies of employment, as the most successful surely will. In this scenario, the forces of market competition will continue to generate organizations that favor leaders who are tough fighters or ambitious specialists, rather than communitarian healers and high priests.

The truth of the vision, though, is that the alpha-male model of leadership has held sway too long, because of the monolithic nature of our corporate empires. Now the New Economy offers opportunities for a renaissance of the clan-type model for which we were designed. Our forebears lived in smallish communities (some anthropologists and psychologists say that 150 is the maximum size of network our brains can keep track of) where one interacted with kin or near kin, using a flexible division of labor and fluid hierarchy. This was facilitated by the dispersed sources of supply that sustained the community—for it is monolithic supply chains that support monolithic hierarchies. Some software houses, consultancies, professional firms, and new tech businesses come close to aspects of the ancestral communitarian model and are doing well by it. They require a different kind of leader, different from those who are selected and elect to fight to the top in the corporate jungle. The qualities of dominance and achievement still matter, but coupled with a more integrative, empowering, and communitarian ethos. This is a truly novel and welcome dimension of the New Economy.

It is often too much to expect all these qualities in a single person, and herein lies the solution that many new businesses are finding—which is the one that prevailed in our ancestral communities: multiple power-sharing leadership. Various leadership partnerships seem to work: the tough fighter who goes out into the world to win markets allied with a wise chieftain who orchestrates the spirit of the community; the visionary enthusiast who works alongside an experienced and authoritative administrator who ensures systems deliver reliably. Many family firms and buddy-founded businesses have enjoyed phenomenal success with such models, such as Procter & Gamble, Hewlett-Packard, and even the mighty Microsoft.

The key is to ensure that the leadership pattern is one that ministers to the two great needs of every community and every business: a viable place in the world and a strong and healthy internal identity.

Nigel Nicholson is chair of the organizational behavior faculty at London Business School and author of six books including *Executive Instinct: Managing the Human Animal in the Information Age* (Crown Business). His research interests are in personality and leadership, risk and decision making in finance, and family business relationships. He consults widely on leadership, culture, and change.

5

The Growth Imperative

Noel Tichy

Growth is risky, but less so than not growing. Growth involves looking at the organization from the outside in, focusing on what customers and the environment require, anticipating changes, and envisioning new products or services. This may mean filling new needs for existing customers, existing needs for new customers, or new needs for new customers. Growth should be aligned with the organization's mission, or the mission should be realigned with new realities. These changes may require transformation of the organization. Growth requires competent people, capable systems, and disciplined leaders who can generate ideas, values, emotional energy, and action and make tough decisions. Growth can be supported with new planning, goal-setting, communication, compensation, and training mechanisms, and recruitment of new talents and perspectives.

E very leader, in any organization, faces the same fundamental challenge. You are given a set of human, technological, and financial assets to manage, with the task of making those assets more valuable in tomorrow's world. In short, if you are a leader, your job is to add value. There are two ways to do that. You can use those assets more productively—deliver more and better goods or services—and you can grow your assets—increase their reach and capability.

Growth usually is seen in financial terms—for good reason in the case of most businesses. If you're competing for capital in the financial markets, you probably have to grow profitably at 12 percent a year and have an operating return on assets of 16 percent a year. According to research by Columbia University professor Larry Selden, that is what it takes to match the performance of the top quartile of companies in Standard & Poor's 500 stock index. Investment capital is necessary to fund new products and services and to provide the financial incentives that top technical and management talent demands. But even in the world of Internet start-ups, companies in the long run need growth *and* profitability. Without growth, the imagination, energy, and investment that companies need will dissipate; without profitability, growth is unsustainable.

Beyond the financial realities, however, growth is important for strategic and psychological reasons. The way you create a vibrant organization is to engage the creativity, energy, and commitment of every member of the enterprise. People need ongoing opportunities to use their skills, try new things, and stretch their limits. Those opportunities are necessary for people to be their best—and are available in sufficient number only when your organization is growing.

A growth strategy is also the best path toward continual innovation. In education, for instance, there has been an explosion of new models and markets for learning, but most of that activity is happening outside of traditional universities—in companies, in communities, on the Internet—where the growth impulse is strongest. If universities don't grow and adapt, they will soon become marginal contributors.

Growth forces you to look at your organization from the *outside in*—focusing on what your customers and the environment demand of you. Too many organizations, unfortunately, are managed from the *inside out*, putting their own practices, policies, or priorities ahead of the needs of customers.

How Growth Spurs Innovation

Trilogy Software, which develops sales and marketing systems for large companies, is charting its own route to growth, and creating powerful organizational innovations in the process. Joe Liemandt, its 32-year-old CEO, dropped out of Stanford University to launch the company in 1990. Today Trilogy has nearly 1,000 employees, and his personal stake is worth close to $1 billion.

Liemandt's growth strategy is simply to hire only star performers. He is successfully competing with Microsoft on campus to recruit the best software talent in the world. At the heart of his employee recruitment and development program is Trilogy University, modeled after General Electric's Crotonville management development center. (Liemandt's father worked at GE for many years, and the former GE chairman and CEO Jack Welch is a close family friend.)

Through his father and godfather, Liemandt saw the impact of stretch objectives, professional development, and open dialogue on workplace performance. But Trilogy takes these beliefs to the limit. The head of Trilogy University, Danielle Rios, has shown that the kinds of programs developed at Crotonville can be pushed much further. Liemandt and Rios work with new college graduates from 8 A.M. until midnight for three months. The students' "action learning" assignment is nothing less than to develop the next generation of products for Trilogy. The program combines R&D and employee development with weekly evaluations of students' values and performance.

The company hires only 1 in 15 of the people it interviews— and invests $13,000 in every hire. Yet any recruit whose values or performance do not hold up during the three-month orientation is dismissed—6 percent of candidates washed out in a recent Trilogy U. class. And while growth is at the heart of Trilogy's culture, Liemandt does not pursue growth at any price. "We will slow growth down if we find that we're getting close to diluting the quality of our people," he says.

The company uses many mechanisms to support its talent-based growth strategy. For example, each new hire must have a sponsor within the company. If a recruit makes the grade, the sponsor is paid a $1,000 bonus; if he or she fails, the sponsor is fined $4,000. Most sponsors own stock options worth millions of dollars, so $4,000 does not threaten their livelihood. But as one who experienced such a loss reports, "It feels awful. People still give me a hard time about it." Looking back at what went wrong, he adds, "We were pushing to fill head count. I got sloppy, hired a kid who wasn't ready, and he failed. I'm never doing that again."

Broadening the Pond

Start-ups like Trilogy can make growth seem natural. They are driven by entrepreneurial passion and incentives and, assuming they survive, have nowhere to go but up. For established organizations, the challenge is to break the mind-set that high growth is impossible in a mature market. Their leaders must make growth a part of the organization's genetic code. Instead of fishing from the same tired waters, they find ways to broaden the pond. The late Roberto Goizueta reframed Coca-Cola's market opportunity by noting that 5.7 billion people in the world consume 64 fluid ounces of liquids a day—and that Coke has only 2 percent of that "share of stomach." That's a very different approach from trying to incrementally grow your market share versus a competitor.

Likewise, in 1995, GE Power Systems' Bob Nardelli drew scant comfort from the company's 50 percent share of the $20 billion market for power generation equipment. He saw that the market was stagnant and that deregulation was creating opportunities for new competitors. Nardelli used the acquisition of Italy's Nuovo Pignone not only to expand GE's presence in Europe but also to enter new market segments in the oil and gas industry. Today GE Power Systems fishes in a $700 billion pond, encompassing the whole value chain of power generation and delivery, from the wellhead to the end user.

The key to such growth is to serve the new and existing needs of both new and existing customers (see figure). Organizations that satisfy themselves just with serving the current needs of current customers inevitably stagnate. The growth matrix suggests three alternative strategies: filling new needs for existing customers, existing needs for new customers, or new needs for a whole new set of customers. These strategies are simple to conceptualize but difficult to execute. They require you to search not just the external environment but the soul of your organization. New market needs can be identified by looking beyond your (and your industry's) current way of doing business, understanding how customers actually use your products or services, and anticipating changes in the market. New customers may be identified in terms of geography, demographic segment, or market segment.

By 1989, Reynolds and Reynolds, based in Dayton, Ohio, had seen the effects of ill-defined growth; 1980s-style conglomeration and overseas expansion had sapped its strength and focus. New

To plot a growth strategy, identify the new and existing needs of both new and existing customers.

	Existing	New
New	D Product and service enhancements and innovation	C Breakthrough ideas and market insights
Existing	A Stagnation	B Geographic expansion or product repositioning

Needs (vertical axis)

Customers (horizontal axis): Existing — New

Broadening the Pond
Source: Every Business Is a Growth Business, p. 90.

CEO Dave Holmes believed growth was still the answer, but with a different approach. Working in a mundane industry (printed business forms) and an uncertain one (computer systems for car dealers), the company moved from Quadrant A to Quadrant D of the growth matrix. Serving new needs of existing customers was the easiest path, and the one most likely to yield quick market insight. Reynolds and Reynolds developed systems that integrate car dealers' sales, parts, service, vehicle registration, document retrieval, and customer follow-up functions. It also provides consulting, training, and marketing services.

Revenue grew to $1 billion in 1996 from $600 million in 1991—with profits growing at a compound annual rate of 36 percent. The company's return on equity exceeds 25 percent.

Holmes supported growth with new planning, goal setting, communications, compensation, and training mechanisms. He also recruited executives from much bigger firms, including Motorola, Procter & Gamble, and Xerox, to bring "new genes" and fresh perspective for the founding-family shareholders who largely set the agenda. With its expertise in information systems management, the company has expanded the pond further to include a new set of customers—physician groups and health care delivery systems.

Lessons from a Nonprofit

Focus: Hope in Detroit understands the growth matrix as well as any corporation. The organization was founded by Father William Cunningham and Eleanor Josaitis in response to the Detroit riots of 1968. The most pressing need they saw at the time was hunger—malnourished infants losing as much as 20 percent of their brain power, which may never return. Focus: Hope's food distribution program became the model for the federal Women, Infants, and Children program and now delivers food to 80,000 people a month.

Cunningham and Josaitis then stepped up the value chain and asked how to keep people off food lines. The answer, of course, pointed to a huge new need—jobs. They scanned the environment and saw an opportunity to train machinists for Detroit's auto makers and suppliers. But they soon realized that their customers, the incoming students, often lacked the math and English skills to run complicated machines.

So Focus: Hope developed a fast-track program that took students from 7th- or 8th-grade math and English skills to 10th-grade level in just seven weeks. The program combines total immersion with tough love—anyone who is late, absent, or on drugs is out. After gaining experience in secondary education, Focus: Hope saw similar needs for yet another set of customers— and founded a Montessori school and teacher training program to serve preschool- and primary school–age children. From there the group created a Center for Advanced Technology that offers associate's, bachelor's, and master's level certification. To prove the value of the training and develop a steady job market for graduating students, Focus: Hope established several for-profit businesses serving corporate clients.

The Limits of Growth

Of course, growth carries certain risks and burdens. That was evident early in 1999 when the share price of Dell Computer dropped nearly 25 percent—and brought other high-tech stocks down with it—because the company missed Wall Street's expectations for growth. (The company grew by "only" 38 percent from the prior year, not the 56 percent investors had come to expect.) That may seem like an extreme reaction, but when your stock trades at an astounding 100 times your per-share earnings, you have to deliver, or face severe consequences. Indeed, Compaq Computer encountered a similar decline, for similar reasons, several weeks later. The failure to meet investors' continuously rising expectations cost CEO Eckhard Pfeiffer his job—despite years of phenomenal growth.

As any business leader knows—or soon finds out—you cannot set high growth targets and then simply wish for the best. You can achieve fast growth only with competent people, capable systems, and disciplined leadership. Leaders have to be prepared, as Joe Liemandt was, to say they will not push growth beyond the capacity of people to deliver the quality that customers demand.

It is possible to buy growth through mergers and acquisitions, as we have seen in recent years. But that strategy, too, has its limits. Ford's acquisition of Volvo, for instance, added several billion dollars to corporate revenues, but that by itself did little to help the people running the F-150 truck or Taurus businesses. They still had to grow their own organizations. Therefore Jacques Nasser, Ford's CEO at the time of the acquisition, drove for a behavioral shift that would permeate the organization.

A one-dimensional obsession with growth also takes a toll on the quality of life for workers, their families, and communities. To sustain any institution into the 21st century leaders balance many competing interests and expand their view of the organization's role in society. For example, Ford's Business Leadership Implementation, a three-day workshop for 55,000 employees taught by 1,500 managers, includes a half-day of community service. Nasser supports that investment because he sees the business benefits of an engaged workforce and because he sees growth—financial, professional, and social—as essential to the company's future.

Role of Leadership

To add value to your assets, you need a vision of where you're taking the institution and a strategy for getting there. You have to paint a clear picture of your destination and the route. That may require a total transformation of the organization, especially when past practices and assumptions forestall growth.

Successful leaders of such journeys are invariably creative thinkers. They know how to look from the outside in, challenge the status quo, move proactively, and spot and cultivate talent.

They translate their vision of the future into what I call a *teachable point of view*. This has four elements:

- *Ideas*—the products, services, markets, distribution channels, or customer segments that are going to be most important

- *Values*—the behaviors and ideals that support those business ideas

- *Emotional energy*—the drive, communicated to others, to create positive outcomes

- *Edge*—an engagement in the business that allows leaders to make tough yes-or-no decisions

All of these are essential to asking the right questions about the future and to formulating and implementing a growth strategy. A teachable point of view, grounded in an understanding of your mission, also helps you know when to say no to people, practices, and opportunities that no longer add value to the work of the organization.

The leaders of Focus: Hope, for instance, adhere to a clear point of view and mission each step of the way—to provide intelligent, practical solutions to poverty and racism, and to respect the dignity of all people. They stay in touch with the needs of the marketplace and are constantly finding new opportunities to add value. Yet they say no to a lot of things. For example, casinos are coming into Detroit, promising to hire inner-city workers. The casinos asked Focus: Hope to train everyone from construction workers to card dealers. Focus: Hope declined, because it would have diverted resources from the group's primary task.

With the death of Father Cunningham in 1997, Focus: Hope also learned that with growth, an organization can flourish even after a leader is gone. Today the 40 managers are learning a disciplined, mission-based budgeting process that is helping them continue to grow the organization.

Trilogy, GE, Compaq, Focus: Hope, and hundreds of other high-growth enterprises are demonstrating another lesson: that when an organization is growing, its people are too. For these organizations, growth is always a tool for accomplishing more, never an end in itself. Their leaders know that growth entails risk, but that growing is less risky than not growing. It is part of the genetic code of all living systems and must become so for all organizations. Like all living systems, organizations that are not growing cannot survive.

Noel Tichy is professor of organizational behavior and human resource management at the University of Michigan and director of the Global Leadership Program, an executive-development consortium of 36 companies. He consults to corporations around the world. His books include *The Leadership Engine* (with Eli Cohen) and, with coauthor Ram Charan, *Every Business Is a Growth Business*.

6

How Managers Can Spark Creativity

Dorothy Leonard and Walter Swap

Most of this century's innovations have come from groups. Leaders can cultivate creative collaboration by creating five conditions: (1) preparation (collecting both expertise and new perspectives); (2) innovative opportunity; (3) divergence (a range of options through professional and personal diversity); (4) incubation (time out for reflection); and (5) convergence (selection of options). Leaders must establish psychological and physical environments that support creativity; they must identify opportunities and set direction.

In today's knowledge economy, we cling to many myths about creativity. We believe, for instance, that creativity is a solitary practice, when in fact most of this century's greatest inventions and discoveries—computer electronics, commercial aviation and space flight, the breaking of the genetic code—have emanated from inspired *groups*. We believe that creativity cannot be managed, when in reality managers can strongly shape the creative process. But perhaps most prevalent—and least productive—is the belief that groups must depend on a few often eccentric individuals for creative output. In reality, any group can become more creative if its leaders understand and support the dynamics of creative collaboration.

Looking beyond these myths, most students of creativity and leadership agree that the two disciplines are deeply related. One cannot thrive without the other. Creativity is a process of developing novel and useful ideas, whether an incremental improvement or a world-changing breakthrough. It encompasses more than the launch of a new product or project team. It is what effective organizations *do*.

Decades of psychological research on human behavior and the work of colleagues such as Teresa Amabile have provided much insight into how the creative process unfolds. It hinges on a repeated cycle of divergence and convergence—to first create a rich diversity of options and then to agree on the best ideas to implement. The process of creativity involves five steps.

• *Preparation.* Creativity may emerge in unexpected ways, but it does not come from the blue. It springs from deep wells of expertise. Research shows that the most creative people have a towering command of a given discipline, and such expertise can take 10 years to develop. But creative groups also need "beginners' minds"—newcomers to a field who bring fresh perspective and ask good questions. Composing groups with both kinds of insight is a key for leaders.

• *Innovation opportunity.* Expertise must be applied to real-world problems and opportunities. Everyday occasions for innovation may take the form of a customer request, a special assignment, or a crisis demanding a quick response. Such explicit demands for change usually dictate the goals or scope of a group's creative endeavor. But often the more difficult challenge is recognizing an opportunity to make a creative contribution in the absence of a crisis or an external demand.

• *Divergence: generating options.* It is difficult to develop creative solutions without having a wide range of alternatives. That breadth of choice can spring only from diversity—of working and thinking styles, professional and personal experiences, education and culture—within the group itself. Generating ideas is the most dynamic and most social phase of the creative process. It often presents the greatest challenge to managers inclined to set an agenda, press ahead, and push people toward an agreed-upon outcome.

• *Incubation.* Probably the worst time to make a decision or address a problem is when we are pressed for an answer. We need time and space to reflect on solutions or considerations that may not be immediately apparent. And time, one of the scarcest resources in any organization, is usually allocated by leaders. One of the neglected skills of creativity, of project management, and of leadership is knowing when to call time out for such reflection.

• *Convergence: selecting options.* If you succeed in assembling a richly diverse group that challenges convention (and one another) with useful ideas, you then must agree on a direction, strategy, or solution. Leaders play many roles in the idea-selection process: referee, coach, lobbyist, diplomat, conductor. But too often we seek quick closure on a solution that may preclude more effective alternatives. The urge to converge is a natural tendency in organizations, especially during times of change. But unless the process is well managed the most vibrant and innovative ideas can be lost. Skillful managers balance the need for a wide variety of options with the necessity of closure.

This five-part process describes, in slightly different terms, five essential skills of leadership—spotting talent, identifying opportunities, assembling teams, allocating time and resources, and setting direction. Leaders are responsible for a creative ecology—the *psychological, physical,* and *organizational* environments in which people work. How we manage each of those three interrelated dimensions of work can nourish (or diminish) the creative life of the enterprise.

Psychology of Innovation

The single most important influence on creativity—and a factor largely shaped by the attitudes and actions of leaders—is the psychological environment. We can strengthen that environment through, among other things, risk taking and failing forward, communicating openly, promoting passion, and building values and culture.

Failing forward. By definition, innovation involves taking a risk. Only leaders who encourage others to distinguish between intelligent failures and stupid mistakes—and who reward the former—are likely to encourage creativity. After all, a lot of scientific inventions, from penicillin to Saran Wrap, have come out of apparent failures.

Consider the case of Dave Fournie, a mill superintendent at Chaparral Steel. Fournie championed the purchase of a $1.5 million magnetic arc saw designed to trim the ends off of steel beams. He won approval for and installed the machine at the mill in Midlothian, Texas. It was a complete failure. The magnetic field that it set up was so strong that it would snatch pens out of one's pocket. Fournie and an engineer spent months trying to make the saw work. Gordon Forward, later chairman but then president and CEO, allowed the nightmare to go on for nearly a year, until Fournie acknowledged defeat and removed it.

What do you do to a manager who invests that much money and time trying to make something work, and finally gives up?

At Chaparral you promote him—not because he failed but because he had a history of success, had taken a reasonable risk with management support, and had tried his best. Fournie learned important things from the experience—one of which was when to shut something down.

In contrast, the CEO of a retail food business urged his senior executive team to develop new ideas to promote the company's reputation and visibility. Taking that charge to heart, an enterprising vice president launched a company Web site in 1997. But when the CEO opened the next board meeting, he was furious, demanding to know, "Who put our company on the Internet? Don't you know that isn't used by anyone except sex-crazed druggies?" Besides a public berating, the astonished VP was given a less desirable, overseas assignment. He promised never again to try anything like it—or, we suspect, much of anything else. Which company values creativity? Which would you want to work for?

Acknowledge the moose on the table. People who cannot communicate openly cannot create much of lasting value. Yet many organizations live with taboo issues that everybody recognizes but nobody will talk about. For example, one CEO—who communicated mostly by memo, kept a close tab on subordinates, and managed only by the numbers—complained that his managers lacked initiative; they in turn felt stifled and undervalued. In that company, the quality of leadership was the moose on the table. In other cases, it might be a project schedule that everybody knows is going to slip, but no one will address in the team meeting. Those kinds of group norms are deadly to creative thought. Whether through gentle humor, outside facilitation, or dramatic organizational change, leaders must be willing to break taboos.

Seek people with a passion for the cause. We used to hire people for their brawn, then for their brains. Now we want their hearts.

Effective organizations engage whole people and try to make their time at work also be time at play. It's no longer enough to match people's skills to a job; we also have to find people who care about what they're doing. Passion is the difference between "You couldn't pay me enough to do this" and "I can't believe I'm getting paid for it." We have all experienced those two extremes, sometimes in the same day. And without passion for the product, the purpose, or the task at hand, it is difficult to generate creative ideas. Effective leaders encourage that passion by attending to the nature of the workplace, the design of work itself, and incentives that support high performers' intrinsic motivation (see "How to Make Good Work Its Own Reward").

Build a creative culture. The most potent message to the organization is its leaders' behavior—especially when things go wrong. What happens to risk takers is far more telling than any pronouncements about collaboration and change. Everyone in Chaparral Steel, for instance, knows the story of Dave Fournie— just as everyone in the food service company knows about its banished vice president. However, modeling creative behavior takes more than rewarding it in others. It means taking risks in our own work that can be explained throughout the organization and making creativity vivid and understandable in our business context.

Exploring Work Space

Creativity requires a lot of interaction, especially during the key phases of divergence and convergence. It also requires times of solitude, especially for the intervening step of incubation. Physical work space can either enhance or inhibit interaction, communication, and serendipity. Chance encounters with colleagues,

How to Make Good Work Its Own Reward

How can leaders encourage the kind of passion for the cause that inspires great creative work? We can start by providing three things most valued by self-motivated people.

- *Autonomy.* The mission and goals of an organization, and the tasks of a particular work group, are usually a given. But the freedom and responsibility to determine how to achieve those goals are prized by high performers—and can be a source of even greater energy and commitment.

- *Time for personal projects.* Companies like 3M and Hewlett-Packard give employees time and resources to explore intriguing projects on their own. They not only encourage serendipity but also renew the personal and institutional vitality essential to the creative process.

- *Opportunities to learn.* One motivator available to all organizations is the opportunity for people to develop new skills and insights. While not all companies can compete on pay and benefits, they can all offer expansive jobs and enriching challenges. Organizing work around cross-functional projects rather than rote tasks, exposing people to new ideas, and providing a variety of assignments are key to sustained learning and excitement.

customers, or alien ideas can spark intuitive thought. With a little (creative) planning, almost any office space can be designed to capitalize on such encounters—and can make them something less than pure chance.

One of the ways to enable interaction among diverse work groups is to create space around "watering holes"—kitchens, coffee pots, or mail rooms—where people tend to congregate informally. Such unplanned encounters would not normally happen in the conference room. Strategically placed reading matter from outside your industry can also help stimulate ideas, and bulletin boards or white boards can help capture them.

Most organizations are architecturally geared toward convergence rather than divergence. Yet even in this most common of business activities—having a meeting—we underestimate the importance of physical comfort and social interaction. Ten-minute stand-up sessions, for instance, are not the way to reach agreement on substantial issues. And spaces that do not easily hold all members of a group cannot facilitate convergence (though they may work fine for divergence).

Accounting firm Arthur Andersen in London has a "chaos zone" with vivid graphics, easily moveable furniture, and a bright red brainstorming room—all of which encourage divergent thinking. An area called "Zen" supports quiet thinking and incubation. A comfortable conference room, along with private office space, allows people to come together and make decisions.

The Idea Factory, a San Francisco creative consulting firm, has a single cavernous room containing a small theater, a cubicle for software programmers, a library of books and magazines, and a quiet meeting space that can be reconfigured to suit the needs of the group. CEO John Kao's office is a corner of the room set off by screens, couches, and a table.

At Fisher-Price, teams of designers and engineers have individual work spaces but also have created a common area with sofas and soft chairs where they meet casually. This area is lined with racks of competitors' toys, which team members study, play with, and use as reminders of the customers they serve and the competitors they face.

However, creating an environment hospitable to creativity need not be an exotic or expensive undertaking. Even when space is at a premium, there are ways to create open space. When Charles Rossotti became commissioner of the Internal Revenue Service, one of the first things he did was to buy (with his own money) some equipment that he felt would encourage communication—door stops. He understood that the unplanned communication that occurs when you have your doors open is an important provider of opportunity.

Environments for Organizational Luck

Why is it that some companies are consistently "lucky"? It has been said that people create their own luck; so do organizations. They prepare for serendipity, recognize opportune moments, and allow people to seize those moments. Leaders can encourage a readiness for the unexpected through their organizations' physical and social architecture, as we have suggested, but such openness must extend to our organizational practices.

Many creative products or services result from *empathic design*—a process in which designers, engineers, marketers, and team leaders immerse themselves in the environment in which potential customers live and work. Proximity to customers provokes unconventional thinking about our organizations' capabilities and potential service offerings.

Likewise, a creative culture is the product of empathic *organizational* design. We must understand how people work and how the organization's practices, processes, and policies either enhance or inhibit creativity. We must nurture what Nissan Design International's president Jerry Hirshberg has called "creative abrasion"—the process by which intellectually diverse people generate, vigorously debate, and ultimately implement ideas. That process can indeed run against the grain of organizations wired for top-down management and quick resolution (or suppression) of difficult questions.

Leaders must give others the latitude to bring in, and protect, individuals who are different in their perspective, background, and experience from those already in the organization. We also must recognize that even a diverse group over time settles into its own routines and can lose its creative edge. We can continually bring intellectual diversity into the group through visitors, internships, job rotations, site visits, and other intellectual stimuli.

We can also help groups confronted by a changing environment to debate and converge on a new direction. One useful exercise for doing so is to first identify three or four *core capabilities*—knowledge assets that provide competitive advantage. It is more difficult than it sounds. Working with a representative group at the operating unit level, ask yourselves:

What knowledge do we possess that has built up over time, is not readily imitated, and is highly valued by our customers?

Is this knowledge superior (not just equivalent) to that of other organizations in our field?

Can we base many products or services on this knowledge?

Is this knowledge likely to remain valuable in the future?

The group should then identify three to five *driving forces* in the environment—social, political, technological, or competitive factors that may affect your purpose and direction. Consider how each force (for example, the rise of the Internet, the aging of the

U.S. population, the growth of global trade and capital) is likely to affect each core capability. As you assess your strengths in light of these forces, you may find new opportunities for action—or find that what was once a core capability is actually a core rigidity likely to impede performance in the new environment.

Such efforts at creative problem solving and strategy making are essential to the work of leaders in the knowledge economy. In today's organizations we usually develop ideas, and create value for customers, through groups. And managing groups means managing creativity. We must bring to the creative process the same kind of understanding we bring to managing the financial assets of the firm. Because most meaningful work is collaborative, our job as leaders is to create environments that bring out every group's highest potential. That may be the most creative work of all.

Dorothy Leonard is the William J. Abernathy Professor of Business Administration at Harvard University. She has taught executive courses at Harvard, MIT, and Stanford and consulted to governments and corporations around the world. She is author of *Wellsprings of Knowledge* and, with Walter Swap, *When Sparks Fly: Igniting Creativity in Groups*.

Walter Swap is professor of psychology at Tufts University. He was dean of the colleges, and he chaired the Tufts Department of Psychology for six years, founded the university's Center for Decision Making, and has conducted numerous management workshops. He is author or coauthor of, among other works, *Group Decision Making* and *When Sparks Fly: Igniting Creativity in Groups*.

7

The Business Case for Passion

An Interview with Randy Komisar

Entrepreneurial leaders are those who defy the common view, who believe that their vision is true and they can make it happen, and who also can learn and adapt to correct their course. They also need to be great communicators to share their energy and vision with potential employees, partners, and investors and to inspire them with the possibility of having a large impact and creating substantial change. Character is the essence of leadership, and leadership is about inspiring and motivating and allowing people to realize the greatness in themselves rather than the leader's greatness.

Author, entrepreneur, executive, public interest lawyer, community development worker, Randy Komisar has worn many hats. A "virtual CEO" of several start-ups, he is a canny observer of Silicon Valley business and culture. He spoke with *Leader to Leader* about leading in the New Economy, understanding risk, and creating new definitions of success for leaders, organizations, and society.

Leader to Leader: As a virtual CEO, you act as an investor, adviser, mentor. What do you look for before signing on with a company?

Randy Komisar: I look for opportunities to work with interesting ideas and great people. My criteria basically are threefold. The people: Do I relate to them and their values? Will they be exciting to work with? The product or service: Is it something I care about, something I am personally interested in? And finally the impact: Is it a big idea? Will it be a viable business? Can I actually help build something that will survive in the market and thereby realize the potential of the big idea?

L2L: Is there a model there for less professional investors? Are the people and their ideas a reliable predictor of success?

RK: This is something that I've debated long and hard. Whether or not there's a clear business model early on, there are certain touchstones that serve investors well. First, since there are certainly no *lesser* returns to doing things that you are interested in with people who you respect than there are to doing things you're not interested in with people you disrespect, choose projects you care about with people who you value. Using different criteria for business decisions than you would use every day as a human being in evaluating an opportunity makes no sense.

The other touchstone is passion: you have a far greater opportunity to be successful with something you're passionate about because you're more engaged and committed. People tend to be tenacious about an idea for one of two reasons. Either they're excited by it or they're fearful of what they may lose if the idea fails. I don't find the latter motivation to be very constructive in terms of the ultimate outcome. So you might as well be motivated by the positive rewards of fulfilling your passions.

L2L: Since you wrote *The Monk and the Riddle*, the bubble has burst on the Internet Economy. How has that changed thinking or behavior in Silicon Valley?

RK: Well, the bubble appears to have burst, for now anyway. What's amazing is what hasn't changed. There are still hordes of entrepreneurs flogging half-baked ideas. There is still a lack of rationality around the real value of those ideas. There is more lip service given to business models and to profitability, but I don't see tremendous insight from the entrepreneurs into what that actually means for their projects. There is clearly a difference in the professional investment community; people are less likely to invest in something that appears to have no fundamental underpinnings. But surprisingly, in areas that point to big new markets—like wireless or infrastructure plays—you will still see investors suspending their own disbelief and charging headlong into the abyss. To some extent, the less they know, the bigger it appears, the more likely they are to take chances. The more you understand, the less you can believe that the overall potential is as big as you need to make the numbers work.

L2L: You talk about the Silicon Valley orientation to risk, which is maximizing opportunity rather than minimizing failure. Explain the difference and what that means if you're the leader of an enterprise.

RK: What it means is—particularly if you're the leader—you go for broke. You never hold back. Because it's the prospect of having large impact, creating substantial change, making a big hit that ultimately excites investors, the management team, and the employees in these ventures. There's no hedging in the start-up game. That is very different from most business because in most established business, if you are a middle or senior manager, the last thing you want to do is fail. Failing can be detrimental both to your career and to your company. In the start-up game, it's quite the opposite—if it isn't something that is big and has the potential for a large impact, that is worth failing at, then it's not worth spending your precious time on in the first place.

L2L: You say 60 percent to 70 percent of success is luck. For investors, that's easy. You build a large portfolio and spread the risk. But how does that translate to a personal or organizational strategy for leaders?

RK: Understand that there's a big difference between smart luck and dumb luck. The principal elements that will determine your success in the long term are not within your control. But that doesn't mean that you are simply playing the lottery. To maximize your opportunity for success, you still need to work very hard; you need to be very smart. But hard work and smarts alone won't ensure your success. You need to take advantage of the confluence of many elements. Your team needs to be as good as it can ever be all the time. There is a premium on excellence. That won't guarantee your success but it will increase the probabilities tremendously when the right elements appear. If you're tenacious enough and your vision is clear enough, ultimately the opportunity for success will arise. Be ready for it.

L2L: What is the key to entrepreneurial leadership?

RK: Entrepreneurial leaders need to be a little bit deaf and a little bit blind. By definition they're trying to do something that defies the common view. They have to be inured to skeptics. They have to believe that their vision is true and they can make it happen. But if they are *too* deaf and *too* blind they won't learn from the market or their advisers, and as a result they won't have a chance to course-correct. They won't be able to respond and adapt as more information becomes available to them. It's a tricky balance.

They've also got to be great communicators. They've got to be electric in sharing their energy and vision broadly among potential employees, potential partners, potential investors. That borders on charismatic. Now, there are different styles of charisma. But there has to be something compelling about the leader that inspires others to follow.

And, whether it's a start-up or not, you need a leader with adequate self-knowledge. Lots of entrepreneurs—especially those who experience early success—don't understand the basis for their success and believe themselves infallible. Those entrepreneurs tend to fail the next time—hard. Without understanding your own strengths and weaknesses, you are unlikely to create an organization with the genetics for success, where each piece complements the rest and the whole is stronger than the parts.

L2L: So it's no accident that many Silicon Valley companies are associated with an individual—a Steve Jobs, a Larry Ellison, a Scott McNealy.

RK: That's right. Like them or not, those people are incredibly brilliant entrepreneurs, and I don't think they're principally motivated by the money. You could argue that Bill Gates seems to crave power and wealth, but the reality is, he has stuck with his company through thick and thin. It is something he started as a youth, and he never talked about his exit strategy. The self-righteousness of Microsoft is an expression of his own beliefs and motivation.

That is very different from the approach of many entrepreneurs today. In the old days "exit strategy" meant there was liquidity for their investors; today it seems to mean you can take the money and run. That's wrongheaded, and it doesn't build good companies and it doesn't speak to great entrepreneurship. Steve

Jobs, Scott McNealy, Bill Gates, Larry Ellison, Andy Grove—these people did not have exit strategies. I can't attest to the purity of their motivations in every case but I recognize the depth of their motivations.

L2L: How do you advise the next generation of entrepreneurs?

RK: First of all, I don't work with the "speed to greed" crowd. If I get a sense that that's your motivation, I simply won't take on the assignment because I'm not going to get any psychic rewards. My advice to those motivated just to build a fat bank account is that it won't serve them well, especially when the market goes through tough times. They are unlikely to sustain the emotional commitment they will need to make it through.

L2L: And what do you tell those who are simply considering a career change?

RK: When I talk with people who are trying to analyze the risk of undertaking a new venture—not entrepreneurs but people joining the management team or staff in the organization—fundamentally, the question is, "Why not?" People often present me with a balance sheet evaluating the risks, the pluses and minuses. It's almost always inconclusive. Opportunities in the start-up environment defy that sort of analysis.

I counsel people to think about different kinds of risks. First you need to consider the risk to your family. If you're at a point in your life where you can afford to lose a gamble and take a chance—you have no dependents, no debt—you may still be overly worried about risk. But that is simply risk to ego.

Next, it's important to consider what risk you're already taking today. Many people don't think about their current situation as a risk because it's knowable. But in reality, they may have already assumed the risk of doing a job that potentially does not excite their passions and does not express who they are, the risk of working with people they may not respect, working in an environment where they may not feel empowered. In fact, these considerations go beyond risks—they become certainties, and they're very negative. Ultimately what is at risk is your long-term satisfaction and happiness. Looking at an opportunity from that standpoint, people tend to feel much more comfortable taking a chance. Not necessarily for financial success alone, but taking a chance of becoming more satisfied. What they're really betting on is the opportunity to engage themselves in truly interesting work with people that they enjoy and respect.

L2L: In the book you describe big-company managers visiting Silicon Valley in hopes of mimicking entrepreneurial culture. You suggest that these efforts are doomed. Why is that?

RK: This is a big, big problem. Most large companies succeed and prosper because they have established policies and procedures designed around managing complex and large-scale operations. It's a very important skill and a critical competitive advantage. But the psychology of creating and managing that sort of operation is 180 degrees off from the psychology of taking risks around launching new ideas. And the notion of being an intrapreneur—somebody who goes into a large organization to be at the vanguard of redirecting or cannibalizing the current business—big companies hate the "C" word—will find that the process and procedures that make the mother ship so successful will do them in.

The two approaches are at odds. But there can be a marriage of convenience. There is a sense that what we're really doing in Silicon Valley is research and development—that by and large, very few start-ups are intended to be viable, independent companies. Instead, they vet ideas, create new technologies, prove out markets and opportunities, build value for the risk takers, and then find their way into well-managed organizations that can truly realize the potential of those ideas. We end up with the Cisco model; Cisco Systems makes lots of investments and acquisitions of small companies at the expense of its internal R&D. It uses the marketplace as a petri dish. Very well, I must say.

L2L: Is that the best strategy for larger or established organizations?

RK: Generally, that's right. The CEOs I speak to in older companies truly understand how to make a profit and operate accountable, relatively predictable businesses. But when we talk about the changes happening in the New Economy—and I don't like that term—they are both fearful and strangely detached. They seem to take cover in the fact that they're approaching the end of their careers and they thank goodness they won't have to wrestle with these big challenges. That is discouraging because these are leaders who, if they were emotionally prepared in the last days of their high-powered careers, could best assume the risks of transforming their organizations.

There's nothing wrong with legacy businesses. I wish I had one—a profitable business that generated cash and gave you independence. There is a big problem with legacy thinking. What we need is new, dynamic thinking applied to legacy businesses to bring them into today's new opportunities.

L2L: And what's wrong with the term "New Economy"?

RK: The problem is the way that we've been using it. Yes, there are many new things about the economy that require us to change the way we think about business. We now have a broad-reaching network that changes the relationship between customers and companies. Communications of all kinds are ubiquitous and instantaneous. We also have increased the speed at which change occurs in business. Those two dynamics define what I think of as the newness of the economy. But when I hear the term "New Economy" applied to business, it's usually an excuse for bad behavior. It's somebody trying to explain why something that doesn't make sense will ultimately make cents. It's a lack of disciplined thinking that is dismissed as, "Well, I don't know, it's the New Economy."

L2L: Apart from sloppy thinking, what worries you about life in Silicon Valley?

RK: We face huge challenges in dealing with the social ramifications of this economic exuberance. There's incredible heart to this Valley that's built around risk taking, change, innovation. I think that this is precious to our economy and to our culture. But all this newfound wealth, much of it being generated without creating any real value or commitment to long-lasting positive change, has led to a culture of opportunism and expedience. I see it gravitating from the business world into the culture at large.

The press is always asking me, "How can you start the next business in Silicon Valley when it costs a million dollars to buy a house? How do you get the next management team to move here?" My response is, Who cares about the next management team; what about teachers? What about policemen? What about the people who are essential to the infrastructure of our society? My concern is that we have failed to recognize the foundation of our success and to respect it.

As I look at kids in this valley, they are living well-appointed lives, but they're not getting a lot of attention. They live in an environment where they're unlikely to surpass the achievements of their overachieving parents. If they don't begin to define success differently from their parents, they are likely to live lives they would define as failures. This is all wrong, and we are not doing enough to mitigate the excesses in this culture and guide the children toward success.

L2L: You have said that business is "the last remaining social institution to help us manage and cope with change." But is business equipped to see us through the changes it's helped generate?

RK: Not now. It's clear that in our society the church as a bastion of spirituality has lost tremendous clout, both in terms of the family and in terms of society. Government is in disrepute, struggling to be relevant. With both of those institutions on the wane, we have to realize that the national religion in this country is now, unfortunately, business. And the problem is that business is not moral. It's not immoral either, by the way; it's amoral. We make it moral or immoral depending on what we bring to the equation. Capitalism is so successful because it asks only two things of people—that they be greedy and that they be aggressive. It doesn't ask them to be altruistic; it doesn't ask them to think outside of themselves; it doesn't ask them to think about society as a whole.

Now, the problem with capitalism being amoral is that if we let these competitive processes just run their course, they don't take into the equation the social costs and social needs. We try to tax those into the equation but that doesn't work well. The way to make business work in the long term is to humanize it, to encourage people to bring their values to their business. I'm saying let's go back and realize that work is about your ability to create, an expression of who you are and what is meaningful to you. Use business as a tool. Bring who you are to business and in the process you will be able both to prosper—as you define it—and to have impact.

L2L: Are there lessons you see that can be shared between entrepreneurial organizations and philanthropic or social sector institutions?

RK: Yes. I worked in the public interest field for years. I moved on to business for a fundamental reason. I found that in too many public interest or government organizations, the high ideals were often undermined by poor practices that belied those ideals.

Silicon Valley was attractive to me because I found a place where the market economy celebrated the importance of people largely because of the value of intellectual property. The bottom line reinforced my ideals. When I look at how the two worlds interact, I see lots of interesting experiments. There are entrepreneurs now trying to create venture funds for social progress. I applaud them for that. But let's make sure that any approach to the public welfare includes more than dollars on its bottom line. It must include the kind of qualitative results that are foreign to the marketplace. Where entrepreneurial and philanthropic cultures come together is at the human level, where individuals in business begin to embrace certain less quantitative and more qualitative social objectives and to find partners in the not-for-profit world to help address them.

L2L: We've talked about the difficulty of old companies trying to learn new tricks. With everyone now trying to figure out e-commerce, what are some principles for success in that world?

RK: I'm actually not as bullish on e-commerce as I am on other aspects of the newer economy. By and large, the ideas in e-tailing tend to be boutique retail concepts. The notion that every business could be reinvented on the Internet on a global basis—that there would be a global supplier of videotapes, a global supplier of books, a global supplier of pet supplies—is absurd. Instead, we've created The Corner Pet Store online or the Corner Video Store online. Many of these are viable businesses, but they are not significant businesses, nor are they big or exciting ideas.

I do think there are aspects to e-commerce that are unique to what you can do online and will fundamentally change things. For instance, eBay created a genuinely new form of e-commerce. It's an exciting idea because it does something, by creating a huge one-to-one network of people selling and buying things, that couldn't have been done before. At eBay the network and its participants are the real assets. It's created a vast marketplace that couldn't be created in the real world.

L2L: Let's return to leadership. You have created an interesting typology for leaders: There's the retriever who assembles a team, the bloodhound who pursues a trail, and the husky who carries the weight.

RK: And the St. Bernard we hope we never need.

L2L: Right. But can leaders ever change into a different breed?

RK: We have created an expectation that the natural development of individuals in the workplace would lead them through all three phases. That they would master each. I think that's wrongheaded. There are exceptions, but not many.

In the past when people have been able to evolve through the critical phases in the life of an organization, they've had plenty of time to do it. Today time has been foreshortened. You almost have to bring on somebody who is equipped to handle the next phase of the challenge before the current one is finished. We need to realize that certain people add a lot more value as entrepreneurs than they will ever add as operating managers. Let them go off and start the next big thing while a new set of operating professionals realize the potential of the maturing venture.

The other thing to consider is, ultimately, what is leadership? People ask if a leader is trained or a leader is born. I think the answer is slightly different. Leadership resides in character. A great example is Nelson Mandela. Here's a man who was put in prison off on an island for some 25 years, basically incommunicado, who ultimately emerged to lead South Africa's transition from apartheid to an open society. There is nothing in the conventional definition of leadership that would predict his success in doing that. Nothing except character.

We think about leaders as having authority, as having control, as having the ability to make decisions. But in my mind, leadership is more about inspiring and motivating. It's about allowing people to realize the greatness in themselves rather than demonstrating the leader's greatness. The best leaders are empathetic. The best leaders have self-knowledge; they are capable of illuminating the potential in those around them. In that sense, the leadership requirements of the newer economy are not very new at all.

Randy Komisar incubates Silicon Valley start-ups and helped launch WebTV and TiVo, among other companies. He is the former CEO of LucasArts Entertainment and Crystal Dynamics, a cofounder of Claris Corporation, and former CFO of GO Corp. He is author of *The Monk and the Riddle: The Education of a Silicon Valley Entrepreneur.*

8

Sustaining the Ecology of Knowledge

John Seely Brown

Three economic shifts create the imperative to generate new knowledge. The first is from conglomeration to demassification, as products, markets, and organizations are broken into smaller, specialized units. The second is from simply making products and services to making sense to stakeholders. Ideas must be compelling enough to change habits and beliefs. One must interpret the forces that drive market change, motivate a diverse workforce, build agile organizations, create a shared sense of place, and foster intellectual capital. The third shift is from established rules of engagement to self-determined ones, driven by the creation of new business models.

Economic and social wealth in the New Economy increasingly depends on rapid knowledge creation. Organizations that create value through new products, services, and ideas will prosper. Those that fail to build the intellectual capacity and personal engagement of their members will stagnate. The generation of new knowledge, largely based on digital technology, is driving three fundamental shifts in the economy, each of which poses strategic challenges for leaders.

From conglomeration to demassification. Most products and services—as well as markets and entire societies—are breaking into smaller, more specialized units. In the realm of products, Moore's Law—which says that the power of integrated circuits doubles every 18 months—now applies to goods in all fields. Because integrated circuits are omnipresent, the distinction between low-tech and high-tech products is fuzzy at best. The performance of almost all products, including cars (which today may need an occasional software tune-up), medical equipment, home appliances, and industrial goods, is improving at breakneck speed—far faster than those products have traditionally evolved. And despite the recent wave of merger-mania, demassification also applies to organizations, which are outsourcing more and more of their work and which increasingly must tailor their products and services to individual tastes. Likewise, in families, schools, and communities, for better or for worse, fragmentation is becoming the norm. Power in the New Economy is shifting to the smallest possible unit.

From simply making products and services to making sense. Increasingly, leaders are becoming sensemakers, whether for customers, employees, or investors. How do you interpret the market? How do you sort out the forces reshaping the competitive landscape? Where might we be at risk as the world and the marketplace change? How do we respond to change? How do we build a marketing plan around latent needs? How do we engage the talents and energies of an often diverse and independent workforce? And perhaps most important for leaders, how do we design a truly agile organization?

As leaders move from making products to making sense, we must focus on the shared sense of place—whether physical work space, online networks, or organizational community—that increasingly defines the quality of work life. In the process of creating these physical and virtual work spaces, we must find ways to foster intellectual capital that becomes inextricably bound to a sense of personal meaning.

From established rules of engagement to self-determined rules. Organizations in every field are seizing opportunities to create new business models. Consider the latest wrinkle in DVD, or digital video disc, technology. Rather than renting a videocassette or standard DVD, which must be returned to the store after one or two nights, the new Divx discs allow you to watch a video and keep it. But, typically, two days after your first showing, your Divx player must get a new password from a central computer and bill you for additional viewings. The future of this technology is far from certain, but it represents nonetheless a dramatic bid to change the behavior of a market. Such changes are evident in every industry, creating a new imperative for organizations to see more clearly, make sense faster, and learn faster than their competitors.

Turning Ideas into Knowledge

These trends may not provide a specific plan of action, but they make clear that the only winning strategy is to engage the full force of the firm in creating new knowledge. Essential to the process of knowledge creation is the adoption of shared beliefs. Any new idea requiring a change of thought or practice must be justified in the eyes of colleagues, customers, and critical stakeholders before those constituents will be willing to act on it. This process is largely social; it depends on the credibility and standing of an idea's champions, the evidence that supports their case, and the way others in the organization or the marketplace respond.

Several years ago, for instance, banks lost a fortune trying to convince consumers to do simple financial transactions online. Today, as technology has improved and our acceptance of it increased, millions of people track and trade their stocks, shop for mortgages, and buy cars online. Such changes do not happen simply because a new technology or "better idea" exists; new technology and good ideas often fail. They happen when an idea is compelling enough to change personal and group beliefs. Any successful innovation must earn the warranted belief—the authority—of others in the community before people will embrace it. It is the willingness to act on belief that matters.

An organization is a knowledge ecology; it is fundamentally dynamic and gains robustness through diversity. But ecologies cannot be designed; they can only be nurtured. The key to nurturing these ecologies is finding the balance between spontaneity and structure. People need both the latitude to improvise and the business processes to apply their knowledge. Thus, creative leaders must learn to be bold yet profoundly grounded. It's easy to be conservative and grounded, or to be radical and impulsive. It's hard to be both grounded and radical (and the literal meaning of the word—"going to the root"—suggests exactly the right approach). That is the discipline of knowledge creation.

My own experiences at Xerox PARC suggest ways to handle the creative tensions inherent in knowledge ecologies. Hundreds of people a year visit PARC and ask, "How do you manage creativity?" The answer is simple: you can't. You can manage innovation. But you cannot manage creativity, only foster milieus that promote it. You let the world do more of the work of creativity for you. That means, for one thing, giving people the freedom to fail and then reflect, because we learn far more from failures than from successes. In the athletic arena, for example, it is inconceivable that anyone who is afraid to fall could become an expert skier.

Nurturing creativity also means understanding the mindsets of those most involved in the creative process—and walking a tightrope between two fundamentally different creative motivations (see figure). A healthy knowledge ecology needs two types of contributors, characterized metaphorically as the serious scientist (analytical, focused, consistent) and the hungry artist (playful, transcending boundaries, unpredictable). How we bring together different cognitive styles largely determines the success of our strategic capabilities.

The perceived barriers between scientists (who move molecules) and artists (who move minds) are overstated. Scientists and artists, who tend to be more inward looking, are highly compatible in the experience of Xerox PARC, as are designers and engineers, who are outward looking.

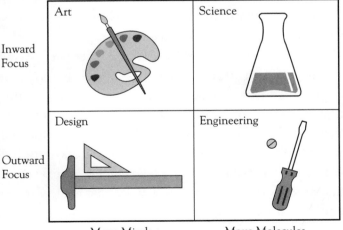

The key is to insist that both types be equally grounded in the mission of the organization. That is the essence of sense-making. With shared understanding of purpose we can ask that people lash themselves to a problem. We must live the problem—connecting with others, listening, and eliciting the cross-currents of doubt, debate, and exploration that surround any new idea. That is how to build a research or a marketing strategy, and how to build a knowing community.

The Sociology of Science

In sponsoring a knowledge ecology, Xerox PARC brought together physicists, sociologists, psychologists, anthropologists, designers, and artists. And in the process, a surprising thing happened. We had always held the traditional view that artists and designers are natural collaborators, as are scientists and engineers. We thought the barriers were between the soft disciplines of art and design on one hand, and, on the other, the hard disciplines of science and engineering. Artists and designers, after all, are trained to move minds; scientists and engineers are trained to move molecules. We were wrong.

It turns out that artists and scientists collaborate naturally, as do designers and engineers. Why? Both scientists and artists are concerned with looking inward. They're pursuing inner truth, self-expression. Can you imagine Picasso conducting a customer survey? Absurd. On the other side of the coin, no designer or engineer can succeed without thinking about the outer world of user needs and desires. The challenge is to devise dynamic structures that bridge these worlds. That is a leader's own creative contribution.

A powerful and largely self-governing structure for connecting people emerges from communities of practice—the entities that actually do the work of the enterprise. Communities of practice are the working fellowships, both within organizations and across common disciplines, bound by shared interests and tasks. For instance, marketing, design, and accounting represent communities of practice that exist in every organization, and often such communities are the source of new knowledge. One mechanism that Xerox has developed enables us to apply the learning of a vital community of practice. The company has nearly 20,000 technical representatives, people who repair our customers' machines in the field, and every day some of them make discoveries. Because machines age differently in different settings, they develop unique histories and unique problems, not all of which can be predicted. So we tried to create a mechanism that tracks these discoveries, combines them in useful ways, and contributes to the company's knowledge (see "A New Law of Knowledge").

We created a Web site where tech reps can post their tips or insights and get quick feedback from their peers. This is far more powerful than simply entering information in a database; it is a way to test new ideas, collect evidence, and mediate discussions electronically. If the peer review team cannot quickly validate or refine the idea, an expert is called who acts as referee, exploring the idea with others and ultimately accepting, improving, or rejecting submissions. Tips that are validated by this vetting process become sufficiently credible that other tech reps can act on them, and are posted for worldwide distribution.

One aspect of this feedback structure was decisive. Every posting carries the tech rep's name, along with the names of

A New Law of Knowledge

Volumes have been written on the nature of the New Economy. At the risk of both hopelessly complicating and oversimplifying the picture, I propose a Newtonian-like "law" to describe the competitive dynamics of the knowledge economy.

The formula given here represents a straightforward proposition: if knowledge equals a belief leading to action, learning is simply the increase of knowledge over time. Sustainable competitive edge, then, can be seen as the differential rate of learning. It's a function of the number of people in the firm who learn differentially faster than competitors. In other words, in a time when both the rate of change and the growth of knowledge keep accelerating, the more people you have who can learn more in a shorter time, the more competitive you will be. I illustrate these forces as follows:

- Knowledge (warranted belief leading to action) = K

- Learning (the rate of change of knowledge over time) = $L = dK/dt$

- Sustainable competitive advantage, or force of the firm (the differential rate of learning) = $F = dL/dt = md^2K/dt^2$ (where m = size of firm)

Such is a metaphoric description of knowledge economy. The real formula for success is less mechanistic; it requires the creative energies of everyone associated with an organization, as well as careful stewardship of an organization's shared purpose and practices.

Created with the help of Sandy Campbell, vice president, special programs, corporate research and technology, Xerox Corporation.

those who refine the idea. Because it is a relatively closed community, people who consistently contribute the best ideas become more central members of their community of practice. In every field, professionals draw much of their identity from their standing in their community of practice.

This process has afforded us an unexpected opportunity to see how social capital is created simultaneously with intellectual capital—and demonstrates the necessity of respecting both. For example, when our managers first began to recognize the value of the tech reps' ideas, their first response was, "This is great, let's reward these postings with cash bonuses." But the tech rep community said, "No, we're doing this because it is important to us." It was the intrinsic rewards that were driving people to share, debate, review, and then make their insights public.

Thus leaders must build systems that support the interplay of social and intellectual capital. It is impossible to do that without the help of the users of the systems. Our process, for instance, was codesigned with tech reps themselves. The key was simply to implement in a corporate setting the social dynamics and values that make science work. These dynamics grow out of the power of the peer review process, the ways ideas gain credibility, and a respect for authorship and reputation.

The Promise of Community

Knowledge creation is not an activity that can or should be confined to the work organization. Indeed, the transfer of knowledge not only within but also between institutions is the subject of debate in both academic and corporate circles. Some organizational researchers, for instance, characterize knowledge as sticky (subject to hoarding and difficult to move); others describe it as leaky (inherently mobile and difficult to confine). But Xerox itself has shown that knowledge can be both. The first personal computer and first graphical user interface (GUI) that led to the Apple Macintosh—and later to Windows—were both invented at Xerox PARC. These inventions did not move beyond our research lab yet found their way to Apple and others who developed and marketed breakthrough personal computer products.

However, this famous "fumble of the future" was not the result of a grand miscalculation or obvious oversight (not obvious, at least, at the time). It was a failure of divergent communities of practice to turn ideas into knowledge that others could act on. Few people in 1978 understood the commercial potential of the personal computer. And PARC's small, eccentric community of researchers was as uncommunicative with outsiders (including engineers from down the hall) as it was inventive. Likewise, most others in the company (whom we as researchers derided as "toner heads") focused narrowly on what they knew best—commercial copiers. It took a then tiny community of practice outside the firm—personal computer designers—to recognize the potential of the personal computer.

Yet even an uncommon ability to coordinate diverse communities of practice is not enough to move from invention to innovation. Organizations play two key roles in that process. The first was articulated by economist Kenneth Arrow 25 years ago: "innovation by firms is in many cases simply a question of putting an item on its agenda before other firms do." And setting an agenda that reflects the skills, capacities, and mission of the organization means recognizing that what is right for one organization may not be right for another. The second task of organizations, of course, is to execute their agenda. Here again, leaders must attend to social patterns and practices, not just to strategy and technology.

Structures for Collaboration

Communities of practice, so essential to knowledge creation within the organization, also sustain and are sustained by the broader community. The personal identity that emerges through community membership is seldom limited to one's place of employment. We all hold diverse and overlapping affiliations—to our profession, avocation, neighborhood or region, political cause, or faith. And all enterprises rely not just on their own employees and suppliers but on many social resources—colleges and universities, school systems, public and nonprofit institutions—for the expertise and infrastructure to operate.

What makes Silicon Valley, Hollywood, New York's financial district, or London's theater district so dominant in their fields are the porous relationships among myriad communities. The flow of knowledge among organizations is as important as the flow within. Partners and competitors live in complex symbiosis; the boundaries between organizations are fluid, and ultimately everyone benefits from the movement of people, goods, and ideas. These centers of expertise are the result of *regional* knowledge ecologies. The dense overlap of shared interests and varied affiliations is what makes these regions so vibrant.

Sometimes regional ecologies spawn conscious collaborations, such as Joint Venture: Silicon Valley, a nonprofit partnership of businesses, government agencies, labor, professional organizations, and foundations. Its conferences and demonstration projects address economic, environmental, educational, and quality-of-life issues affecting four counties and 2 million people.

Whether or not they develop such formal efforts, all regional ecologies create their own social architecture—structures and cultures that allow members to both construct and consume knowledge. One of the most powerful of these structures is the

Internet. No other vehicle provides the reach and reciprocity needed for knowledge sharing across geographical, organizational, and professional boundaries. The Internet *augments* rather than replaces the kind of shared space and work practices inherent in a region and essential to a knowledge ecology.

Just as no one manages the Internet, no one can manage a knowledge ecology. But we can understand the working principles of our communities, adapt our roles to be more effective, and improve the tools that support creativity. In the knowledge economy, therefore, management gives way to mission. It is people's commitment to the continuous generation of knowledge that gives life to the communities on which we all depend.

John Seely Brown is chief scientist of Xerox Corporation and director of its Palo Alto Research Center (PARC). Brown has helped shape corporate strategy and has expanded the role of corporate research to include such topics as organizational learning and workplace ethnographies. He is cofounder of the nonprofit Institute for Research on Learning, has edited the book *Seeing Differently: Insights on Innovation*, and coauthored *The Social Life of Information*.

9

Making the Leap to Internet Time

Patricia B. Seybold

*Developing e-business is harder for large, established compa-
nies than it is for start-ups. Several steps are involved: (1)
focus on brand recognition, rather than creating a new entity; (2) have different leaders focus on different sets of targeted customers, interactions, or distribution channels; (3)
pull together customer information—who your customers are
and what interactions they've had with you; (4) if separate
divisions have their own Web sites, use cross-functional co-
ordination to create a unified architecture and navigational
system; (5) anticipate the questions that customers will ask
and make sure the information is waiting in the back-end systems; (6) communicate the vision and manage change. A
human resources person on the team can pave the way for
appropriate organizational changes.*

One of the most difficult tasks leaders face is trying to keep
up with the blistering pace of Internet time. We are all
prey to it. If we don't adapt our companies to Internet time,
we're likely to be out of business in no time.

Organizational inertia is not simply a matter of scale. Any
established organization—large or small—has difficulty moving
quickly and changing course quickly.

Over the years, leading my own company and working with many other firms, I've learned some important things. First, as philosopher and business thinker Fernando Flores told me, leaders should not expect organizations to change overnight. Organizations are made up of people. People's nervous systems take three years to learn new behaviors that supplant old ones. Organizations can't change faster than people can learn new ways of dealing with them. That may be one reason why Internet start-ups are able to evolve quickly, while established companies seem to move at a snail's pace. When you're in start-up mode, you're free to experiment and try new things. Once you're set in your ways, it takes longer to learn.

The second tip I discovered on my own. Connect all the people in your company to direct customer input and feedback. Those who interact with customers directly can evolve quickly to meet customers' needs. Those people who are insulated from direct customer interactions take longer to see the light. How many people get e-mail from customers? How many people in your organization talk with customers directly on the phone? Who gets product feedback and customer satisfaction ratings? Unless you organize your company so that everyone is bathed continuously in customer feedback, you're going to have a hard time moving fast.

Developing large-scale e-business initiatives is certainly harder for large, established companies than it is for start-ups. Several common issues tend to slow these companies down, even when they want to launch aggressive e-business strategies and to move in Internet time.

Questions for E-Business Strategists

Most of the companies I work with have Internet religion. Their top executives have recognized that not having an Internet strategy puts them at a competitive disadvantage. They need to craft a strategy quickly, and they need to execute that strategy in Internet time.

These are the biggest difficulties such companies run into: How should they organize their e-business projects? How should they coordinate these activities across product lines and divisions? How should they fund their e-business projects? And how can they move quickly when there are so many players who have to be moved along, communicated with, sold, seduced, and brought in? All of these companies already have Web sites; many have *lots* of Web sites. They have already made progress in developing corporate standards for a common look and feel across the company's disparate Web sites and a strategy for linking all the different customer-facing sites to a common corporate home page. But the next steps are daunting:

1. *Crafting an Internet business strategy.* How will we make money on the Net? Should we build a portal? Should we build a "dot-com" company and spin it out as an Internet IPO? What do we do about our channel partners? Should we sell direct? If so, how do we change our compensation structures?

2. *Designing an e-business strategy.* E-business is not only about the Web! Customers want to interact with companies through multiple channels. They call our various call centers; they send us e-mail messages and faxes; they shop in stores. They buy through retailers, dealers, and resellers. We need a multichannel approach to our customers. Who will pull this together?

3. *Organizing for success.* Having a small, focused team is the way to do things quickly in Web time. But who gets to be on that team? Where do they report in? How should they coordinate with the rest of the organization? Who will take leadership? Will they get support and buy-in from the rest of the firm?

4. *Pulling together customer information.* We don't have our customer information in one convenient, easy-to-access place. We have different pieces of customer information scattered all over our enterprise. How do we present a coordinated face to the customer if we can't tell who our customers are and what interactions we've had with them? Who is going to "own" the customer information? How will we ever reach agreement across departments, divisions, and business units?

5. *Evolving our Web sites.* Each of our separate product groups, divisions, and marketing departments has designed Web sites to focus on different products or audiences. Should we evolve these into a single seamless set of offerings, or should we have very distinct "places" on the Web for different products or audiences?

6. *Reconsider our back-end systems.* We spent time and money on Y2K compliance. We've just finished a major enterprise-wide systems installation. Now we have to reengineer all of these systems again? Our Information Technology department doesn't "get" the Internet. We'll have to continue to work with outside consultants and system integrators to do these e-business initiatives. How much is it all going to cost? Where's the return on investment?

7. *Communicating the vision and managing change.* We keep growing through acquisition. We do things a certain way. We're going to be changing a lot of policies and business processes. We probably need to change our compensation structures to at-

tract new talent. We're going to need people's buy-in and co-operation. If we ram this down their throats, it's doomed. Remember what happened with Project X, Initiative Y!

Crafting Your Internet Strategy: Focus on Your Brand

There are no easy prescriptions for each of these issues. The "right" answers are probably different for every organization. But I see glimmers of useful approaches.

Building an Internet business from scratch and designing an e-business strategy are two separate undertakings. Most companies have them confused. If you want to launch a new business on the Internet, then do it as an Internet start-up. If you want to take your existing business onto the Web, take your cues from your existing customers.

If your organization has a strong brand presence in the market today, think long and hard before you decide to create a new branded entity on the Web. With 1,000 new portals and storefronts opening on the Web every day, building a brand presence is going to be tough and expensive. Can you afford the $100 million or so it may take to build a new brand? What's wrong with the brand you already have?

If you do decide to launch a new Internet business and brand, then do it as a separate business. Don't encumber it with the overhead and business processes your established business units "enjoy." This is a business development decision and will need an Internet-savvy businessperson to run it. Don't plan your revenues around advertising (ephemeral) or profit margins on existing products (difficult—the Net will squeeze them). Instead, focus on new business models. How can you offer a brand-new product or service that is only made possible via the Web? Or how can you reinvent an industry, given the Net?

Designing Your E-Business Strategy

Existing companies need to start with existing customers. Don't focus on all the new customers you might acquire via the Internet. Focus on how you can use the Internet, kiosks, and customers' handheld devices (cell phones, pagers, and so on) to make it easier for your current customers to do business with you.

The Internet is usually the catalyst that propels you to map out an e-business strategy. But don't limit your strategic thinking to the Web. Design a multichannel strategy even if you choose to implement first on the Web. Start with customer support. Move on to electronic commerce. Make sure that you give customers all the information they need to actually make a purchasing decision. Streamline the research, buying, and delivery process, then move on to personalization and community. A lot of companies don't bother getting the basics right. Then they wonder why their grander strategies fail.

Remember, the key to success is simple. Your goal is to make it easy for customers to do business with you. A successful e-business strategy is a multichannel strategy. The Web is one, albeit key, ingredient in the recipe.

Organizing for Success

Top executives focus on targeted customers. The companies that have been successful in honing e-business strategies often began by having a high-level executive who focused on one target set of end customers (consumers and small business customers, high-net-worth customers, frequent travelers, enterprise accounts). This visionary business leader assembled a team of key managers, each responsible for an interaction channel (Web, call center, e-mail, kiosk) or a distribution channel (financial advisers, agents, wholesalers). American Airlines, Bell Atlantic, Charles Schwab, Hertz, and Wells Fargo all took this approach.

If you begin by focusing on a single customer segment you can later expand your strategy to include additional sets of customers.

A small team drives the effort. How many people should be directly involved in your e-business effort? In a large company, so many are involved that it's difficult to keep the team small and focused. To compound the problem, you often hire one or two large consulting, system integration, and design firms, each with its own small army, and before you know it, you have an unmanageable project.

Ideally, you don't want more than six or eight full-time people reporting to the business leader sponsoring the effort. Their job is to own the customer experience for the target set of customers who use their channels of interaction. They will, of course, be working with others. But as a team, they work together and come up with a coherent, cross-channel strategy.

The skills you're looking for on this e-business team are a hybrid of customer support, marketing savvy, and technical architecture. Among them, the people on this team need to have deep knowledge of your existing products and processes, your customers' needs and expectations, and the architecture of your back-end systems. It is important for the technical architects to be an integral part of the business team, not just recipients of a set of wish lists.

This is the core team that maintains the customer focus, sets the priorities, designs and monitors the metrics, and makes

demands on the rest of the business to revamp underlying processes in order to meet their customer experience goals.

A larger group does the implementation. You will undoubtedly
have a much larger group implementing the technology infrastructure, designing the Web sites, developing integrated voice
response systems, creating call center scripts, interfacing to back-
end systems, and preparing and organizing content and databases.

Outsource development—cautiously. It's common practice to
outsource the development of much of these initiatives. There
is lots to do and very little time. However, be careful not to outsource too much. Again, small is better. A handful of senior architects and developers will be able to deliver better results than
a small army of young hotshots.

Don't outsource your intellectual property. In particular, maintain control over all the architectural decisions. Do your own
customer scenario design and carefully specify the navigational
choices. Consolidate and manage your customer information
internally. And maintain control over your content inhouse.

It's surprising how often big companies outsource the creation and maintenance of their product and marketing information. You need to establish in-house procedures for crafting
information that fits customers' needs. What's the task the customer is trying to perform? What kind of information does someone need at that point? What offers do you want to be able to
make in different contexts?

*How do you organize across product lines and customer
sets?* What if you want to have several different business groups
targeting different customer sets? Unless there's really no overlap among customer sets, you run the risk of creating business
processes and back-end solutions that aren't in synch. However,
if you do a careful design up front, you may be able to pull it off.

The key is for all of the different customer-advocacy teams to work together (weekly meetings advised) and to develop a single underlying architecture of services. This means that the technical architects on these teams need to be a single virtual team, working across their respective customer-centered teams.

The key is always to start with the customers—to understand their needs and to appropriately shape their experience of your brand.

Consolidating Customer Information

The massive problem of fragmented customer information often leaves project planners in a state of paralysis. Either they can't begin to consolidate customer information because each product group owns—and wants to control—its own information, or the company has been product-centric and not customer-centric, selling through channel partners and never actually collecting much information about its end customers.

The customer information problem is a political problem. What everyone is waiting for is for someone with enough authority—the CEO or the Executive VP level—to simply dictate that, from now on, there will be a single customer profile for each customer, with all related information linked to it. Once this mandate has been issued, everyone will find a way to make it happen. The top executive who wants to get an e-business strategy moving needs to know that the most empowering step he or she can take is to mandate an integrated approach to customer information.

Start over with the Web. One of the most successful ways to break the logjam on the intransigent customer information problem is to use the Web customer database as a new starting point.

Microsoft did this very successfully as it moved from a product-centric to a customer-centric culture. The first thing Microsoft did right was to charter someone—Pieter Knook—to design a single customer database that would sit behind Microsoft's myriad customer-facing Web sites. This became the interactive marketing database for the company. Knook worked with each of the product-focused groups that "owned" different parts of Microsoft's Web site and with the different marketing groups, each of which was targeting a different customer community (developers, chief information officers, users of different products).

When Knook started this project in 1997, there were 72 different places on Microsoft's Web site where customers' e-mail addresses were being captured. He met with each Web team, gathered their requirements, and then convinced each one to use both the single customer database that his team was designing and also the templates and tools his team developed—templates that would make it easy for Microsoft's Web creators to solicit customer information and have it flow directly into a single customer profile database. That database became the unifying force, because it had the freshest information and because customers could see and maintain their own customer profiles. Eventually, customer records were linked to other databases and applications. That work continues to this day.

Evolving Your Existing Web Sites

Many large companies have multiple customer-facing Web sites, each one created and maintained by a different marketing or product group. The first effort that most firms make is to mandate a set of common design standards for the look and feel of these Web sites, as well as a set of site naming conventions. As anyone involved in this kind of activity knows, this is like herding cats. Getting groups to adhere to common standards for graphic design and layout is hard enough. (Usually this is something people in large companies are used to; after all, we all use the same logos and corporate standards for many other documents.)

The really hard part is setting and enforcing standards for site behavior and navigation. Typically, these Web sites have been built on different back-end platforms, using different technologies and approaches. They may use different authentication mechanisms, different search engines, different e-commerce engines, different personalization engines, and so on.

Single architecture: single behavior. As long as you put up with different architectural choices being made for each of the underlying Web services in your environment, you are doomed to present a fractured, confusing experience to your customers, prospects, investors, and other stakeholders. Your customers will feel more comfortable if all of their Web experiences "feel" the same.

It's fine to vary the "look" of customer-specific Web sites. Teenagers like clutter. Businesspeople want clarity. Browsers need to browse. Task-focused customers want to do what they came to do and get off quickly. What's not OK is to give each of these types of people a different way of doing things. Every car needs a brake pedal, a transmission, a steering wheel, and a set of windshield wipers. Imagine how it would feel if you had two different ways to slow your car down in traffic or two different ways of turning the wipers on and off, depending on which way your car was facing. You want customers to feel comfortable driving your Web site, not confused.

What does this mean? You need to create a common branded customer experience (and a common architecture) across your focused Web sites. For a highly distributed organization, this may

How Will Your Industry Be Transformed by the Internet Economy?

Whether your enterprise sells to consumers or to other businesses or is a nonprofit or government organization, the rules of your game are changing. Much of that change has been catalyzed by the use of the Internet. Customers are demanding increased transparency—in pricing, inventory, logistics, and business policy. Customers now want to "see into" your business to make better decisions affecting their businesses and their lives.

While detailed customer knowledge and trust lay the groundwork for industry leadership, you also need to be willing to cannibalize your own products and practices. It's the players who reinvent their industries—focusing on customer convenience—who will lead the pack in the 21st century. Here are some of the major industry transformations occurring today:

Consumer Financial Services. Online brokerages began the industry transformation. Now that transformation is rippling through banks, insurance companies, mortgage companies, loan providers, credit and debit card companies, and a slew of non-banks (automobile companies, grocery stores, computer manufacturers) are vying for consumers' trust and assets. The winners in financial services will be those who focus single-mindedly on their customers' needs for impressive returns, customer control, and convenience.

Whole Goods Manufacturers. The manufacturer of any product is now responsible for owning the customer's total experience with its brand and its products. Many business and consumer customers want to buy direct from the manufacturer. Customers often expect these products to be custom designed to suit their individual needs. And they want more control over the logistics relating to their purchase and delivery. To succeed, manufacturers will need to forge direct relationships with the buyers and end users of their products while ensuring that their products are distributed and serviced through the channel partners with whom customers choose to deal.

Retailers. Customers continue to browse, shop, and try products in physical stores. But today's customers often do their competitive research, price and feature comparison, and buying online. Whether they shop online, at the store, or from a catalog, customers expect the retailer to recognize them, know their preferences, and reward them for being loyal customers. Internet-only retailers have set the bar for clicks-and-mortar retailers. Customers want to know whether a product is in inventory and to receive the product they purchase the same day or the next. To be successful, bricks-and-mortar retailers will become seamless clicks-and-mortar retailers. To compete, virtual e-tailers will need nearly unlimited inventories, procurable in real time, with immediate, accurate delivery and easy returns processing.

Commercial Services. Commercial banking, insurance, real estate brokerage, advertising, management consulting, and public relations are all under pressure. More companies are outsourcing their non-core competencies to experts in their respective fields. Yet customers aren't willing to be locked into their service providers, nor to pay a premium. To succeed, commercial service providers need to provide best-of-breed, cost-competitive solutions that can hook easily into customers' existing systems. They need to ensure that the complete business process, of which their service is an integral part, is easy to monitor and manage. And they need to make sure that their service can be easily replaced with another, while ensuring that customers are so satisfied by the quality, convenience, and value of the service offering that the switch never happens. *(continued on the next page)*

Government. Local, state, and national governments are all under pressure to provide better services to their citizens and business customers. One of the biggest challenges facing government organizations today is how to cost-effectively provide one-stop shopping across departmental and jurisdictional boundaries. Citizens and businesses want to be able to pay their fees and taxes—and obtain services—easily, no matter which agency collects the fee or provides the service. The government organizations that succeed in providing better services will do so by interlinking their services transparently across jurisdictional boundaries.

Education. Distance learning is transforming the field. So is a renewed focus on the student as the customer. A third change is increased parental involvement in children's education. Finally, the Internet has made it possible for professional educators and specialists in a variety of fields to share research and best practices, develop curricula, and measure outcomes.

Like today's retail establishments, traditional bricks-and-mortar schools (particularly colleges, universities, and other postsecondary institutions) are being challenged by virtual universities. To succeed, schools need to combine the best electronic classrooms with the best on-campus and real-world experiences. They must also provide students with access to all the administrative and academic resources necessary to become educated and certified in their field.

Nonprofit Organizations. Charitable organizations, both religious and secular, will continue to thrive in the New Economy. Yet, like their business counterparts, they will be radically transformed. To meet donors' expectations they'll need to become much more focused on delivering service to actual end customers with as little administrative and marketing overhead as possible.

Like all businesses, nonprofits can use the Internet as a catalyst to streamline internal operations by focusing on a target group of end customers. They can also use the Internet to vastly improve service delivery, to deliver a message to the rest of the world, and for recruiting new donors, sponsors, and volunteers. Nonprofits need to keep detailed, confidential customer profiles of the customers to whom they are providing services and be able to measure and report on the outcomes of those efforts.

be one of the hardest initiatives to pull off. You'll need visionary leadership on the business side with unwavering support and a technology visionary whose instincts are very good.

Information Infrastructure

Redesigning your customer-facing systems (Web sites, integrated voice response systems, call centers, kiosks, e-mail, and mobile alerts) won't be easy or cheap. But what better way to drive your information technology priorities than to start from what has most impact on your customers?

The good news is that you can evolve your back-end systems fairly simply using today's "middleware" technologies. Your goal should be to design your customer-facing front-end systems so that they are making small, focused requests of the back-end systems. Examples might be: "Show all flights from Boston to Chicago leaving after 10 A.M. next Monday that still have seats available." Or "What's the status of my last order?" Or "Do you have that hat in my size in blue?"

The biggest architectural issue you're likely to encounter will be how to give tens of thousands of customers access to the information in your back-end operational systems without bringing those systems to their knees. Your design goal is to anticipate the kinds of queries that customers will be making and to ensure that the information they need is already waiting for them.

What's the budget? Because e-business initiatives are no longer distinct from the rest of the business, it doesn't necessarily make sense to segregate these budgets. Yes, you need to fund the e-business. Yes, you need to build Web sites and revamp other customer-facing systems. And no, you don't want to slow this process down by going through long budget approval cycles. But remember, if you're moving your entire business to an e-business—and ultimately you must—about 70 percent of your IT budget will eventually be driven by e-business priorities. Cisco Systems understands what this means. The IT department reports to Doug Alread Sr., VP of customer advocacy. And all IT projects are justified on the basis of how they improve customer satisfaction.

Communicating the Vision and Managing Change

Most of the groups I've worked with in large organizations have an HR person assigned to the e-business team. The HR role isn't to put the brakes on but rather to see what issues are arising and to pave the way for the appropriate organizational changes. The most typical issues involve changes in job descriptions, compensation structure, commissions, and channel strategies. Other issues involve governance, gaining top executive buy-in and sponsorship of key initiatives, centralized versus decentralized decision making, and cultural diversity.

Get your customers to direct change. What's the most powerful change management tool you have? Your customers! Bring them in. Get them to design their own scenarios of how they want to interact with your company. Listen to their complaints and frustrations. Amplify every customer contact you have. You can't do e-business initiatives in a vacuum. You need your customers to drive this process.

Even if you think your customers aren't Web-savvy, you can ask them how they'd like you to streamline your dealings with them. What interactions take too long? Where are the black holes? When do they get angry, frustrated, and confused? Customers may not say they want to do business online. But they will tell you what they don't like and how you waste their time. They will give you a clear set of marching orders. All you have to do is listen and amplify.

Don't keep customer input and feedback isolated in a small group. Every employee in your organization needs real-time customer input and feedback. Bring customers in to redesign scenarios and workflows. Take a page from Schwab's book. Build a usability lab and bring customers in every day to test every customer-facing design or prototype you're working on. Do this for every channel of interaction: Web, voice response, touch screen, call center scripts, and so on. Make sure that the folks developing these systems and interfaces participate in these usability lab sessions or at least watch the videotapes.

Don't get frustrated when you can't do all of this within nine months. Most of the leaders I've chronicled have been at this for four years, and they're still hacking away at major issues, like consolidating customer information, dealing with channel partner conflict, and so on. Remember, organizational change takes time—all the more reason to get started now. Find a business sponsor, select a target customer set, and get started. Designing and implementing an effective e-business strategy is the most compelling and rewarding challenge for any leader concerned about the future of the enterprise.

Patricia B. Seybold is the founder and CEO of the Patricia Seybold Group (www.psgroup.com), a worldwide strategic e-business and technology consulting firm. Her research, consulting, and executive workshops have widely influenced e-business practices. Her most recent books are *Customers.Com* and *The Customer Revolution.*

10

The Residue
of Leadership

Why Ambition Matters

James Champy

The larger the scale of change, the more likely it is to succeed. Large organizations have antibodies that kill incremental change. Great leaders have ambitious visions marked by a great sense of purpose and a capacity for meaningful change. By clearly articulating what they want to accomplish and the values by which they will do it, they provide the energy and inspiration that engage others. Creators see opportunities that others do not. They begin with a fresh insight, discovery, or conviction and invent the future. Capitalizers scan the environment, recognize and seize an opportunity, and grow it. Consolidators are professional managers who step in, often when an enterprise is in trouble.

We live in a time of extraordinary possibilities. The barriers of geography and ideology are falling. Our markets are becoming increasingly open—goods, ideas, and investment dollars move freely around the world, making businesses everywhere more effective. And new technology, at home and in the workplace, is creating powerful new channels of commerce and communication. Never in work or personal life have so many people had such opportunities to innovate.

Yet ours is also a dangerous time. Since the days of Adam Smith we've assumed that the advance of technology would spread wealth to all reaches of society. That is not always the case. Times of technological change are also times of economic and social dislocation. As we move deeper into the new economy it is wise to examine how wealth is generated and shared, and whether we are using this opportunity wisely.

The dual forces of open markets and ubiquitous technology are reshaping entire industries with breathtaking speed. In the 1990s managers talked about reengineering business processes, and many now believe that effort has run its course. However, the discussion today isn't just about *process* change, it's about a change in our business *models*—how we conceive, construct, and sustain the enterprise itself (see "Tall Ambition: Making an Industry Click"). In this context—fundamentally redesigning work—the age of reengineering has barely begun.

Tall Ambition: Making an Industry Click

In traditional business models—so-called "bricks and mortar" business—strategists are asking how to move from the old ways to something fundamentally new. The question is how to keep the current business running—which after all earns the revenue that allows us to innovate—even as we move to a new business model.

Leaders of the auto industry, for example, are trying to transform the way they build, distribute, and sell cars. The inefficiencies of the current system are enormous. According to a recent study,

---

$81 billion in unsold inventory sits idle in the lots of automobile manufacturers, distributors, and dealers in the United States. If manufacturers were to sell directly to consumers—the same way that Dell sells computers—they could take $54 billion of that inventory out of the supply chain. Yet sitting between customers and the manufacturer are distributors and dealers who, in the New Economy, add little value to the painful process of buying a car.

With such powerful incentives, the shift to a new business model is inevitable. But who will lead that transition in the years ahead, and how will they shape the new business model? They will have to solve the riddle that has plagued today's generation of e-commerce retailers: how to create value in electronic distribution channels. E-commerce today is based principally on price, and no one wants to be in a business where the game is just to drive prices lower. Those who learn to make their offerings distinct—and thereby profitable—will truly reinvent an industry.

While the opportunities are great, to respond to the challenges the new enterprises face will take extraordinary ambition. General Motors and Ford are laying the groundwork for Internet-based, build-to-order selling. Some ambitious start-ups, including Wayne Huizenga's own AutoNation, have also taken the first steps. We are likely to see 10 years of upheaval in the auto industry. As with any great challenge, ambition will be critical for managing through the change.

For leaders, one of the lessons of the past decade is that nothing great ever happens without a great ambition. To gauge the likelihood of success for any change initiative, I've learned to ask, What's the nature of the leaders' ambition? What is their vision of the organization's future? Does the leadership team have an appetite for change? I have found that the larger the scale of the change that leaders seek, the more likely it is to succeed. However, many leaders, particularly in large organizations, are incrementalists. They believe that the safe way to get somewhere is to change a little at a time. Yet too often tiny steps get you nowhere at all. And large organizations frequently contain antibodies that kill every incremental change.

Every great leader begins with a great dream. Ambitious visions not only require a capacity for meaningful change, they also provide the energy and inspiration to engage others. These tasks—articulating a dream and rallying others around it—are the essence of leadership. The study of leaders in every field tells us that leadership is the residue of ambition.

The Path of Ambition

To be sure, ambition needs a better reputation. In recent years, to "be ambitious" has come to be seen as a character flaw. Yet for leaders to make a difference—and for the benefits of markets and technology to be widely shared—requires more, not less, ambition. Great leaders have an ambition marked by a greater sense of purpose, an urge to create something beyond oneself. Whether to provide the best product or service in the industry or to eradicate childhood disease, their ambition extends beyond the accumulation of wealth or power.

Today ambition and achievement can rise and fall with unprecedented speed. But a look at the great achievers of history, and at dozens of business and social heroes of today (from Michael Dell to Sam Walton to Rosa Parks), shows that great ambitions follow a predictable path. People climb the path at different rates;

some rise higher, others fall faster. But almost invariably, they trace a three-part arc of ambition.

• *Ascending the arc.* The first stage is deeply personal. It begins with a fresh insight, discovery, or conviction. Ambitious people are steadfast—and sometimes unrealistically hopeful—in pursuit of their vision. They prepare themselves to recognize, and then seize, the opportune moment.

• *Finding balance.* To succeed, leaders must engage others in the organization or community in achieving their vision. It is here, where high goals are tempered by disciplined execution, that many stumble. We must weigh the risks of underachieving against those of overextending. And we must deliver on our promises and espoused values, or risk losing credibility and the commitment of others.

• *Passing the torch.* It's not easy to give up control of one's life's work. But the best way to keep control is to share it. Passion and commitment are cemented when decision-making authority and personal rewards are widely distributed. Dispersing leadership (and wealth) also helps us recognize when it is time to change our role, reinvent our organization, or step aside for the next generation.

The Nature of Achievers

Ambition, like leadership, is dispersed among people in all walks of life and is realized at different times and circumstances. For some people, like Michael Dell, success comes in their 20s; for others, like Sam Walton, it comes in their 40s and beyond. Yet despite their diverse backgrounds and accomplishments, high strivers usually fit one of three archetypes of achievement. And, while all achievers must pass through all three stages of ambition, their strengths are most evident at different points in the arc. Ted Turner and Wayne Huizenga, for instance, are *creators*. They see opportunities that others do not. Before he launched CNN and throughout his career Turner was told that he would fail, but he proved himself a great trend spotter. Huizenga saw the opportunity to combine local trash-collection companies. By 1984, well before its current woes, his Waste Management had become a $1 billion business and the largest trash collector in the United States. He then did the same for two other fragmented industries—video stores and car sales and rentals—building Blockbuster and AutoNation, respectively. Creators excel in the first, ascending stage of the arc.

They are followed by *capitalizers*, people like Ray Kroc and Sam Walton, who scan the environment, seize an opportunity, and grow an idea. Kroc sought the ideal restaurant for the average person (and he didn't invent McDonald's, he discovered it—because he was looking). Sam Walton wanted to deliver extraordinary value to consumers and built up an existing retail chain to create Wal-Mart. Superb at execution, capitalizers come into their own in Stage 2 of the achievement process, creating balance.

At the final stage come *consolidators*—professional managers who step in, often when an enterprise is in trouble. Al Dunlap, the discredited turnaround king of Scott Paper and Sunbeam, represents the "dark side" of consolidation; on the other hand, Lou Gerstner, who helped revive an ailing IBM, can be seen as both a consolidator and a capitalizer.

The strengths of creators, capitalizers, and consolidators vary, as evident in the different stages of ambition at which they flourish. Yet all ambitious people share a set of personal characteristics (see "Seven Ways to Elevate Ambition"). They show remarkable persistence, preparation, clarity of purpose, and, most of all, optimism. They overcome roadblocks and obstructions. Ambitious leaders may wish for divine intervention, but, in fact, their timing runs as hot and cold as anyone else's. The difference is in how they deal with adversity. They see every setback simply as temporary and external to their own efforts. They never give in to doubt and say, "This was a mistake, I'm in trouble." Nor do they delude themselves about the immensity of the challenges they face. Rather, they prepare for success with single-minded devotion to their cause. They understand the risks they face because they've walked in the marketplace and examined their work and themselves.

Describing your vision and articulating the values by which you hope to attain it are crucial for bringing an ambition to life. The first step is to define the end state that you want to create—whether an incredibly efficient distribution system for computers or a society with equal opportunity for all. Once you state your purpose, however, employees, customers, and communities will hold you to it.

Ambition in Organizations

Organizations tend to be cautious by nature. Large corporations, in particular, develop immunities to innovation, entrepreneurship, and ambition. They train people in the analysis of risk but focus on avoiding the unknown rather than taking prudent chances. They tend to look backward rather than forward. If those who assess risk have no ambition, they will see only the hazards and never the opportunities. And although any organization can succumb to the tragic flaw of arrogance, large organizations tend

Seven Ways to Elevate Ambition

No ambition is likely to draw others to it, or sustain itself for long, without appealing to a great sense of purpose. A noble calling—relieving suffering or improving the environment—is the highest expression of moral purpose. But more commercial undertakings can also assume a greatness of purpose. Leaders can do at least seven things to help people look beyond themselves in pursuit of a dream.

• *Achieve excellence in whatever you do.* Individual achievers—artists, athletes, adventurers—usually excel in their chosen field. They seek recognition for high performance and recognize others' achievements. Being the best at what one does is a deeply held aspiration that transcends the individual leader. Especially if they found or become the prime mover of an organization, they establish excellence in product or service quality as a high purpose.

• *Create great value.* High achievers understand the connection between quality and value. They see that social and economic value is created through effective execution. A company like Wal-Mart creates value through efficient systems that save customers money. A great nonprofit takes pride in the number of lives changed as a measure of its value creation.

• *Empower the individual.* High achievers find ways to attain their dreams, exercise their potential, and exceed previous limitations. Enlightened leaders also give colleagues the information, authority, and resources to make their own decisions on behalf of customers. But an even higher sense of purpose is possible when people join to empower *customers*. Apple Computer, for instance, has always striven to build simple machines that help people learn and be creative. That sense of shared power has seen the company through difficult times.

• *Improve the human condition.* Millions of health-care professionals, teachers, religious and social workers, and public workers dedicate themselves to improving the lives of others. Occasionally an extraordinary individual—a Mother Teresa or a Martin Luther King Jr.—assumes an almost mythic standing. But leaders of such businesses as Ben & Jerry's or The Body Shop make human service an explicit part of their mission—and contribute a share of the profits to the public good. And the stated ambition of Monsanto's Robert Shapiro was nothing less than "to feed the world."

• *Create fun and pleasure.* Effective leaders appeal to a sense of enjoyment as well as purpose in their colleagues and customers. Entertainment companies find a natural link between purpose and pleasure. But leaders like Southwest Airlines chairman Herb Kelleher make fun and good-heartedness essential parts of their organizational culture and strategy.

• *Invent the future.* Great dreamers and doers strive to change the world. Thomas Edison, Guglielmo Marconi, and Jonas Salk did just that. Today thousands of Internet start-ups, biotechnology firms, and social ventures are inventing new ways of doing business and rallying people to a cause.

• *Improve the environment.* Every human activity and organization exacts a price on the environment. One way to elevate one's cause is to make a point of promoting conservation, mitigating damage, and raising awareness. Tom's of Maine, for instance, uses only environmentally benign ingredients—and its respect for the environment is integral to its mission.

to discount a new idea—no matter how great—simply because they believe that it's too small for them. Of course, initially it usually is.

For instance, every large telecommunications firm from AT&T to Deutsche Telekom missed the two most significant opportunities of the 1990s—cellular technology and the Internet. They could have owned these technologies years ago but are now paying fortunes to buy their way in. These companies missed the market because their leaders thought the emerging technologies would be insignificant compared to their current business.

That is why organizations need to cultivate ambition. The only way to create something new and substantial is to have a substantial ambition. General Electric Chairman Jack Welch recognized that when he gave promising young managers "popcorn stands to run"—a small part of the business in which they could act out their ambition and begin to develop as a leader and role model.

Ambition can be developed in an organization, but it must be held first by senior executives in the enterprise. And, if the organization is to be more than a collection of ambitious individuals, its leaders must be able to articulate a shared, compelling purpose and must engage others in its pursuit. In sharing their dreams, leaders encourage others to dream, and to perform. Wal-Mart, for example, is successful because—even years after Sam Walton's death—his passion for value and service is still honored by its frontline staff.

Learning from Failure and Success

Of course, even with the right personal and organizational resources, ambitious people sometimes fall short. The marketplace is fickle and unforgiving. Not every purpose is great enough to engage others. And strivers usually sell ahead of their capability; an early employee of Microsoft, for instance, later admitted, "We sold promises." But when you sell too far ahead of your capability, you can stumble badly.

Achievers must also fight certain impulses that run as deep as ambition itself—hubris and greed. A lot of aspiring millionaires are drawn to the world of Internet start-ups, for instance. Many of them truly want to change the world; some, however, measure their goals solely in terms of the dollar value of an initial public offering. No great business has ever developed out of pure ego or avarice.

Great achievers learn to temper their ambition with self-reflection. They remain true to their values, see the world (and themselves) clearly, and effectively manage the resources that can limit the pursuit of a dream—time, talent, and momentum.

Everyone has the desire to accomplish something great. Unfortunately, most people, starting in childhood, are discouraged from dreaming, or at least from talking about their dreams. One of the great things an organization can do is to help people give voice to their dreams, and provide the means by which people come together to create something greater than themselves. It is the gift of leaders to release the aspirations of others.

Markets and technology change, but ambitious people have faced the same challenges for generations. We have the means today to spread success more broadly than ever before. However, the dangers of failing to spread opportunity are also great. How well we meet that challenge will depend on how wisely and well we use our innate ambition.

James Champy is chairman of Perot Systems' consulting practice and is widely recognized for his work in organizational change, strategy, and leadership. Former chairman and CEO of the consulting firm CSC Index, he is coauthor of *Reengineering the Corporation* (which has sold more than 2 million copies), author of *Reengineering Management*, and coauthor with Nitin Nohria of *The Arc of Ambition*.

11

The Challenge of Strategic Innovation

Costas Markides

A study of small companies indicates that their success is due to capitalizing on shifting market trends or new technologies and creating new strategic positions in their industries that allowed them to compete by being different from, rather than trying to be better than, their much larger competitors. Established companies spend time and energy trying to improve or protect the strategic positions they already occupy. They are weighed down by structural and cultural inertia and reluctance to abandon the present for an uncertain future. Yet there are ways in which they can compete: focusing on the most potentially profitable lines of business and divesting others; identifying new or unexploited customer segments; identifying new consumer needs and filling them; and finding new ways of producing, delivering, or distributing products or services. Leaders can use three tactics to promote innovation: questioning the status quo—even when it is profitable—and searching for new avenues of performance; monitoring strategic health; and cultivating internal variety by experimentation.

Everyone loves an underdog. Unfortunately, most of them fail despite the support from the sidelines! But can we learn anything from the battles these underdogs fight? In particular, can we learn from those few that defy the odds and actually win against much bigger competitors? A study of 30 companies from eight countries, in industries ranging from financial services to food processing, suggests that we can (see "Global Movers and Shakers"). All were small companies that went against formidable competitors but managed to quickly grab a significant share of the market, without the benefit of a technological innovation.

For example, Komatsu attacked much bigger competitors in the earth-moving equipment business—competitors such as Caterpillar, John Deere, and J.I. Case—and still managed to increase its global market share from 10 percent to 25 percent in under 15 years. Gannett Company launched *USA Today* in 1982 as the first national newspaper and, despite facing a crowded field (1,700 daily newspapers), managed to become the top-selling newspaper in the country by 1993 with more than 5 million copies a day. Direct Line, launched in 1985 to sell car insurance by phone, signed 2.2 million policyholders in ten years and became one of Britain's largest car insurers. Starbucks Coffee grew from a chain of 11 stores and sales of $1.3 million in 1987 to 280 stores and sales of $163.5 million in just five years.

What these underdogs achieved is remarkable. The question is, How did they do it? and What can we learn from their success?

Creating New Strategic Positions

The answer, I believe, is simple: these companies achieved so much so quickly because they created *new* strategic positions in the business. Instead of attacking established competitors in their existing (and well-protected) positions, these innovators created totally new positions that allowed them to play the game in a different way.

Global Movers and Shakers

A four-year study of strategic innovation—employing 100 London financial analysts—looked at the performance of companies that, in 10 years or less, achieved significant market share gain at the expense of established competitors, without the benefit of major technological breakthrough. The analysts identified many such companies. The following short list of 30 innovators was studied in depth:

The Body Shop (United Kingdom)

Canon (Japan)

CNN (United States)

Dell (United States)

Direct Line Insurance (United Kingdom)

E Trade (United States)

EasyJet (United States)

Edward Jones (United States)

Enterprise Rent-A-Car (United States)

Federal Express (United States)

First Direct (United Kingdom)

Home Depot (United States)

IKEA (Sweden)

Komatsu (Japan)

Lan & Spar Bank (Denmark)

Leclerc (France)

Medco Containment Services (United States)

Migros (Switzerland)

MTV (United States)

Nucor (United States)

OM Exchange (Sweden)

Perdue Chickens (United States)

Rosenbluth Travel (United States)

Southwest Airlines (United States)

Starbucks (United States)

Swatch (Switzerland)

Timex (United States)

USA Today (United States)

Virgin Atlantic (United Kingdom)

Wal-Mart (United States)

Consider, for example, how Canon managed to challenge Xerox's dominance in the copier business. In the 1960s, Xerox had put a lock on the copier market by following a well-defined and successful strategy. Xerox decided to go after the enormous corporate market by concentrating on high-speed, high-volume copiers. This effectively determined its distribution method: a direct sales force. At the same time, Xerox decided to lease rather than sell its machines, a strategy that had worked well in earlier battles with 3M.

The Xerox strategy was well-defined, with clear boundaries. Throughout the 1960s and early 1970s, Xerox dominated its market and maintained a return on equity of around 20 percent. It was so successful that several new competitors, including IBM and Kodak, tried to enter this market by adopting similar strategies. Fundamentally, their plan was to grab market share by being *better* than Xerox—offering better products or service at lower prices. Neither of these corporate giants managed to make substantial inroads in the copier business. Rather than create a distinctive strategic position, they tried to beat Xerox at its own well-established game.

Canon, on the other hand, chose to play the game differently. Having determined in the early 1960s to diversify out of cameras and into copiers, Canon decided to target small and medium-sized businesses while also producing desktop "personal copiers." Canon also decided to sell its machines through a dealer network rather than lease them, and competed on quality and price. This strategy succeeded: within 20 years, Canon emerged as the market leader in number of copiers sold. It did so largely by creating a *distinctive strategic position* in the industry. Today, having established a strong market presence, Canon is directly challenging Xerox at the top end of the lucrative corporate market.

Competing by Being Different

Canon's position grew to undermine Xerox's own unique position and so erode Xerox's basis of profitability.

This kind of attack is quite common: new strategic positions emerge all the time for many reasons. Changing industry conditions, ever-shifting consumer preferences, new technologies, and new regulations give rise to new opportunities and new ways of playing the game. Alert companies (such as CNN, Dell Computer, IKEA, Nucor Steel, Southwest Airlines, and Swatch) identify and exploit these opportunities quickly. Established companies, on the other hand, usually spend their time trying to improve or protect the strategic positions they already occupy.

Market leaders' efforts are aimed at becoming *better* than competitors, and little or no emphasis is placed at becoming *different* from competitors (see figure). It is rare to find an established industry player who is also a strategic innovator—a fact that hints at the difficulties of risking the sure thing for something uncertain. Compared to new entrants or niche players, leaders are weighed down by *structural* and *cultural* inertia, internal politics, complacency, fear of cannibalizing existing products, satisfaction with the status quo, and a reluctance to abandon a certain present for an uncertain future.

Yet, despite the obstacles, there is hope. Consider these two examples:

• In 1989, when Denis Cassidy took over as chairman of the United Kingdom's Boddington Group plc, the company was a vertically integrated beer producer, with a brewery, wholesalers,

Playing the Game Better		**Playing the Game Differently**
Focus on your existing strategic position and try to improve it incrementally. Practices such as restructuring, refocusing, process reengineering, quality programs, empowering employees, and the like all aim to achieve this.	**Versus**	Identify new or unexploited customer segments (a new "who"); new customer needs that no competitor is satisfying (a new "what"); new ways of producing, delivering, or distributing your products or services (a new "how").

To be successful, a company must be able to do both!

Two Views of Strategic Positioning

and pubs throughout the country. In the next two years, Cassidy set about transforming the company into a "hospitality" organization. The brewery was sold and the company diversified into restaurants, retirement homes, and hotels while keeping its portfolio of large managed pubs. "The decision to sell the brewery was a painful one, especially since the brewery has been part of us for more than 200 years," Cassidy explained. But the move created enormous shareholder value—especially when compared with the strategies adopted by other U.K. regional brewers.

• In 1995, the low-cost brokerage firm Charles Schwab had almost no Internet business. Three years later, its Web site supported more than half the company's total trading volume and about one-third of its total customer assets. Originally started as a separate internal venture, its electronic channel (e.Schwab) was quickly integrated into the rest of the organization so that a uniform product and price were offered to the customer, no matter what distribution channel the customer chose to use (phone, branch, Internet).

Both stories are examples of strategic innovation: a fundamental reconceptualization of what the business is about, which in turn leads to a dramatically *different* way of playing the game in an *existing* business. They tell us that strategic innovation is not the natural birthright of small companies alone.

Leaders as Strategic Innovators

There is no reason why established organizations cannot embrace new strategies. As a leader, if you know that your strategic position will eventually come under attack, or that changes in the environment will threaten your standing, then your motivation is strong to be the one that develops the new strategic position.

Given all the obstacles to innovation that established organizations face, leaders play a decisive role in promoting innovation. Without strong leadership from the top, it is unlikely that an established company will innovate. Effective leaders can use three tactics in particular to promote innovation in their organizations.

• *Jolting the status quo.* The ability to question fundamentally the way a company operates, even when it is profitable and successful, is the most critical prerequisite for strategic innovation. A company must be willing—at the very least—to embark on a voyage of discovery: to question its present status, to be dissatisfied with its latest achievements, and to search for new avenues of performance.

Unfortunately, advising companies to question their way of playing the game and think of alternative ways—especially when they are successful—will not do the trick. Even though few managers disagree with the need to fundamentally question the way they do business before a crisis strikes, few actually do it.

The reason is simple: what gets done in organizations is not the important things but the urgent ones. Questioning one's business, though important, is not seen as really urgent unless a crisis strikes. This is where strong leadership comes in: creating a sense of urgency even when the organization is doing well.

What strong leaders seem to know is that it doesn't matter how actively you question your way of doing things. "Successful" organizations inevitably fall back on old habits. Relative stability, satisfaction with success, managerial overconfidence or even arrogance, monolithic culture, strong institutional memory, and internal political coalitions all breed a dangerous complacency and passivity. This implies that every few years something must happen to stir things up and destabilize the system all over again. What is needed is not so much continuous improvement—that should be a given—but periodic and unpredictable shocks to the system.

Successful innovators are willing to disrupt a smooth-running machine because nobody knows beforehand when exactly the system needs this shaking up. Witness, for example, what Jack Welch did at General Electric over the past two decades: In the early 1980s, he took GE through a massive and painful restructuring program—a challenge that earned him the nickname "Neutron Jack." The restructuring was a success, transforming GE into one of the most admired corporations in the United States during the 1990s. Then, in late 1997, just when GE was posting record operating margins of 14.5 percent and a stellar 25 percent–plus annual return on equity, Welch announced a massive new restructuring program. All of GE's manufacturing units were placed under review to determine how to significantly cut costs and improve productivity. All units and in particular the industrial businesses such as motors, transformers, and locomotives were expected to propose massive cost-cutting measures such as layoffs, shutting down of unprofitable plants, wage cuts, and work transferred to nonunion plants and foreign locations. According to analysts, GE was restructuring not because it was facing losses but because it aimed to become an even leaner and more formidable global player.

Another positive shock can be the arrival of a new leader who is not constrained by the past and is ready to challenge the status quo. Examples abound: Walter Haas at Levi's, Denis Cassidy at Boddington's, Harry Cunningham at K-Mart, Colin Marshall at British Airways, Lou Gerstner at IBM. Even Intel's decision to exit the memory chip business was taken after Andrew Grove asked CEO Gordon Moore to consider what a new management would do if he and Moore were replaced.

• *Monitoring strategic health.* A second tactic used to create a sense of urgency in a well-established organization is to monitor not only its *financial health* but also its *strategic health*. Doing so allows innovators to introduce change in their organizations long before a crisis hits.

Measuring the financial health of a company is simple: you can examine your profitability, revenues, market share, and other financial indicators to get a good sense of your performance. Unfortunately, historical numbers—though necessary and useful—can be misleading indicators of a company's future. There are countless examples of companies that appear to be very profitable (think of IBM in 1990), only to find themselves two or three years later in a crisis. Conversely, many companies that appear to be in financial difficulties (IBM in 1994, for example) are ready to embark on a period of growth and profitability.

Effective measures of strategic health act as early warning systems: they alert you two or three years before a crisis arrives that you need to take corrective action. A few of the most useful indicators:

- Customer satisfaction
- Employee morale
- New products in the pipeline
- Distributor and supplier feedback
- Quality of management, assessed by multiple sources
- Strategic fit of the organization relative to the industry
- Financial health of the organization relative to competitors

However, it is one thing to get an early warning that trouble is brewing and another thing to decide what to do about it and then do it. That is the value of strong leadership: being able to "see" a different future and then having the courage to abandon the status quo for this uncertain future.

• *Cultivating internal variety.* The biggest obstacle to innovation is often the uncertainty surrounding a new idea. The problem is that, even after questioning its assumptions and exploring new possibilities, a company does not know which of its bright ideas will turn out to be a winner—nor does it know which of its current core competencies, if any, will be most relevant in the future. Therefore, advising companies to build their core competencies or to be willing to take the risk with new ideas simply raises the question of which core competencies to build and which new ideas to bet on.

If you are Revlon, how do you know that the Body Shop's idea for environment-friendly cosmetics will catch on? If you are IBM, how do you know that Dell's idea of selling personal computers direct to individuals will be a winner? The simple answer is, "you don't." The problem with good ideas is that you can tell that they are good only after the fact. This implies that you should be willing to experiment with new ideas and see if they work out. What characterizes successful strategic innovators is their willingness to experiment and learn. At any given time, a thousand experiments are taking place, all of them within certain accepted parameters and all of them at the initiative of an individual. Out of this experimentation, winners do emerge—that is, practices and products that customers themselves choose as winners. These winners soon become part of the organization's portfolio. Losers, on the other hand, are quickly laid to rest.

Strategic innovators let the outside market decide what is a winner and what is a loser. No central planners try to outsmart the market. Instead, managers encourage multiple bets (that is, individual initiatives). This process is not necessarily efficient— it requires a measure of organizational slack and internal variety. Competing teams may work simultaneously on similar ideas, or look outside for essential services, or locate far from existing operations. Like the capitalist system itself, this approach can be criticized as "wasteful"—but it is the best engine of progress that we know.

A Model of Innovation

A good example of an organization built for strategic innovation is the Leclerc group in France. Leclerc was founded in the late 1950s by Eduard Leclerc, who decided to give up a career as a Catholic priest and start a supermarket dedicated to offering branded products at cheap prices. The organization has grown to a chain of more than 500 hypermarkets and is now expanding into overseas markets.

Leclerc is able to balance several conflicting forces: it has achieved low cost and differentiation simultaneously; it is highly decentralized and yet well integrated; it has small, autonomous units but still enjoys the benefits of size; it is structured as a federation of independent stores yet behaves as a coordinated network; it encourages continuous experimentation with new concepts yet survives the inevitable losses with minimal pain; it has employees who act like "owners" of the organization yet own no stock; it is values-based, yet is a money-making machine. How does it manage all this variety?

First of all, Leclerc is not a single company. Each store is operated by individual owners who choose to trade under the Leclerc name. But they are not franchisees: they do not have to pay for the right to trade under the Leclerc name (in fact, they receive numerous other benefits from their Leclerc association for which they pay nothing). However, they do have to abide by certain norms—the primary one being that they will never be undersold by competitors. In addition, no individual—including members of the Leclerc family—is allowed to own more than two stores.

Each store has total autonomy over its affairs. It determines what products to sell, what prices to charge, what promotions to run, and so on. In addition, each store can find its own suppliers and negotiate its own prices. This decentralized decision making encourages experimentation and achieves differentiation. But each region has its own warehouse (owned by the member stores), which orders 20 percent to 30 percent of each store's goods on behalf of all its members. In addition, a central purchasing department identifies potential suppliers and negotiates prices with them. Stores do not have to use any of the recommended suppliers but can achieve purchasing economies by doing so. Use of the Leclerc name by all also achieves advertising and promotional benefits and cuts costs. Finally, new Leclerc stores are always started by current Leclerc employees who receive financial backing and guarantees from current Leclerc store owners. The financial backing of a prominent local businessperson has inevitable benefits in dealing with banks for start-up capital.

In addition, every store owner is active in the management of the whole organization. They attend monthly regional meetings as well as frequent national meetings where decisions are taken and experiences exchanged. Regional presidents, who serve as volunteers for three years, handle administrative affairs, visit individual stores to offer advice, monitor plans, and transfer best practices. Furthermore, at the end of every year, each store owner has to distribute 25 percent of the store's profits to its employees.

In this system, the two primary mechanisms of control are a common and deeply felt vision that sets the parameters within which each member store operates and a strong, open, and egalitarian culture. Each store has a unique culture (created primarily by the personality of the store owner), yet a shared Leclerc culture of accepted norms and values allows autonomy and differentiation to coexist with organizational coherence and market power.

Like the market economy itself, Leclerc has created internal variety (which can be considered inefficient) and has allowed the "market mechanism" to separate winners from losers. This is not easy to do. It can be construed by employees and investors as a confused strategy. This is exactly the reason why strong leadership is so important.

In the end, organizational culture is the basis for strategic innovation. *When values and mission are explicit, structures, policies and strategies need not be.* Organizations need to continuously search for new strategic positions *while* moving forward in their current positions. They have to continuously challenge the basis of their existing business and the assumptions that govern their current behavior. Strategic innovation can happen only when we question our way of doing business today and open our mind to new possibilities.

Costas Markides is professor of strategic and international management at the London Business School. He has written on strategic innovation and corporate restructuring in numerous journals, including *Harvard Business Review* and *Sloan Management Review*, and is author of *Diversification, Refocusing, and Economic Performance* and *All the Right Moves: A Guide to Crafting Breakthrough Strategy.*

12

The New Merchants of Light

Harriet Rubin

*Leaders who want to discover new markets or radically trans-
form their industries need to think in new ways. They need
to see that ideas and imagination can have an impact beyond
that of information. Imagination is seeing into the darkness.
Five techniques from history's great leaders can stretch imagination: (1) sit down before the facts as a little child (do not
let them limit or control you); (2) know how the imagination
works (powerful ideas are simple and clearly expressed, democratic, and evocative); (3) use triggers of the imagination
(e.g., writing in poetry rather than prose); (4) to know what
you think, see what you have to say (reality often echoes
words); and (5) understand that the imagination demands
the commitment of your body as well as your mind and soul.
Treat every surprise not as something to be controlled but
something to be accorded respect.*

M ost leaders are capable of much more than even their best
products or management innovations reveal. Leaders
have their own glass ceiling. They face-savingly call it "the top."
But the top is just another boundary. They know there is more.

The urge to accomplish more, to find meaning—in short, to
leave a legacy—is fueled by an inescapable social phenomenon:

137

A generation of boomer executives is marching toward retirement. But instead of becoming tired and resigned, most are becoming bolder. As they approach the high point of their careers, leaders are wondering how their lives' work would be summed up *now*, not in 20 years. They are asking themselves if they are going as far as they are able and are taking on big enough challenges. When you have invested your life in business, the next question is, Did I get out of that investment everything I could?

The answer cannot be found in the daily stock tables. But a new reading of history and literature offers leaders a relevant—and radical—perspective on creating a legacy.

Elizabeth I presided over an England that led the world in the last half of the 16th century, prospering in diplomacy, wealth, and a culture named for her—Elizabethan—that gave birth to no less a figure than Shakespeare. Francis Bacon, the brilliant 17th-century essayist and adviser to Elizabeth and her successor, puzzled over what made his age golden. In his essay "The New Atlantis" he imagined a new utopia had replaced the original paradise that sank. It had no borders, no boundaries. In place of politics, vision ruled. Who was at the heart of this New Atlantis? Not Elizabeth herself. Not even the world's great playwright. Those responsible were the great merchant traders and capitalists of the Renaissance—business leaders who plunged their personal wealth and reputations into ships that sailed beyond where all maps ended. They "sail into foreign countries," Bacon wrote, "under the names of other nations [did he mean corporations?] and bring us the books and abstracts, and patterns of experiments of all other parts. These we call Merchants of Light."

They invested in a mission to bring back greater wealth: new possibilities, plants and spices, fabrics, ideas. They were the first intellectual capitalists. Unlike today's intellectual capitalists, they didn't focus on trying to discover merely what they didn't know. Their interest was not in information: market projections, manufacturing numbers, or trend lines. Their interest was in the imagination. The first intellectual capitalists sailed beyond the known ends of the earth. Business today doesn't go half that far. The intellectual capitalist pursues information in the elements of a soup can or a bar code. He focuses on what he doesn't know. But that's a dry and dreary realm. Imagine how far you could go if you uncovered *what you don't know you don't know*. The original Merchants of Light could see into distances most could not.

Leaders who want to discover new markets or radically transform their industries or perhaps test their own mettle need to explore uncharted waters. They need to sail into the imagination. That used to be reserved for artists and actors and writers, but it cannot be their sole province anymore. Leaders need to think and act not just out of the box, but out of the ballpark. Some already recognize this need and are searching out the tools of the imaginal mind.

The New Intellectual Capital

Business leaders think they know what risk is. But they seldom experiment with "the facts" to realize greater possibilities. We have seen leaders in public life who live for what they don't know they don't know. Gandhi had an extreme and wildly imaginative idea: to free India from British rule, not through bloodshed, but with the enemy's help. Martin Luther King Jr. behaved as if he were leading a Second American Revolution—to free

African Americans. Richard Nixon had the brazen idea of declaring a war on cancer which only now, 30 years later, is showing signs of victory.

For a leader to realize his genius, he must think in different ways. Not one of the captains of industry I'd worked with in 20 years as a publisher and editor had ever ventured far from the known. I searched to find a Merchant of Light. Then in the summer of 1997, one found me.

He had pioneered a new medium in communications and had just retired at age 44 from a stunningly successful business he'd built. He'd reached the top of his game, but wanted more. Information had led him to the top, but ironically that now looked like a dead end.

"I've climbed Everest," he said. "I've sailed in bad weather. I've built a Fortune 100 business. Now I want to do something *really* dangerous. I want to write a book—not to make money, not to build my profile but to understand who I am, what I think, and what I've done. If I survive that process, I figure I'll be ready for anything."

I used to describe the creative process in terms I had heard a young actress use on opening night of "The Tempest." She had made her debut opposite the great Patrick Stewart on Broadway. As applause rained down on her, she hushed the crowd and said, "I want to thank my husband for making my reality a dream." She didn't say, "making my dream a reality"; for great performers, that is easy. The executives and thinkers I worked with had come to see how ideas and the imagination could have an impact beyond that of information. Their ideas had changed businesses and lives. This Information Age pioneer, as close to a true merchant of light as I'd ever seen, was asking for help not to write a book but to learn to use the tools of the imagination.

Searching for More

It was only the first such request I had that summer. I had calls from other leaders—big thinkers—who wanted to go further. Phil Knight of Nike said to me, "My biggest fear is that a few years from now I'll hold a grandkid on my knee and she'll look up at me and ask, 'Grandpa, what did you do when you were young?' I'll say, 'I started Nike.' And she'll say, 'Nike? What's that?'"

Such leaders were implicitly saying, "There has to be more: Help me find it." They had learned to climb career ladders into the stratosphere, but suddenly the rules of the game had changed. Climbing wasn't enough. Doing the obvious or the necessary wasn't enough. A leap was required. "What do you do when you get to the top of the 40-foot ladder?" Zen masters ask. One answer: Let go. Or, more strangely: Keep climbing without the ladder. In other words, do what you can't do.

Socially and economically the late-20th-century emphasis on information is shifting in favor of the imagination. Businesses will be transformed by people as daring as Merchants of Light who see into the dark unknown, who travel into the tunnel at the end of the light.

Leaders who suddenly see the end in sight have to deal with an uncomfortable truth: that a single-minded belief in information may have stunted their abilities by emphasizing only the known or the unknown.

They are craving what the imagination can give them: freedom, the power to take on risk, the ability to work as artists, not just as managers or leaders.

When leaders play in the realm of imagination, they align themselves with creators of the highest order. Lincoln was a writer as much as a politician. So was David, the ancient desert king who transformed a nomadic tribe into a world power in a single generation. David was a poet and musician; he used the imagination as consistently as he mastered martial art and strategy.

These days businesspeople want a remission from ordinariness, much the same as artists. One major investment banker recently said to me, "I always wanted do big deals. Now I want to do deals that are elegant."

Five Uses of Imaginative Capital

In introducing leaders to the imagination and the rewards of imaginative capital, I rely on techniques from history's great leaders who have mastered the imaginal mind. Here are some of those techniques:

1. *"Sit down before the facts as a little child,"* as Thomas Huxley wrote. The facts do not have control of you; your imagination does, and it need have no limits. Real heroes can let the facts transport them to a totally imagined—and far more powerful— state. Consider the case of former naval commander James Stockdale. In 1965, he was one of the most decorated warriors in the armed services. Fearless. Brilliant. Respected. But in one minute he went from being an air wing commander, master of all he surveyed, to the lowest form of life in North Vietnam: a prisoner of war. During a bombing raid his plane was shot down, and as he bailed out from the burning wreckage into enemy territory, he uttered this phrase: "Epictetus, here I come." A strange thing to say as you drop into a state of utter catastrophe.

Stockdale knew the facts would kill him: he was in enemy hands, and his captors were making his survival close to impossible. Only his imagination would save him, as it had saved

Epictetus, a slave in ancient Athens. Epictetus realized that as long as he believed himself free, no one could imprison him. Epictetus had been the young Stockdale's philosopher hero.

So when Stockdale's captors asked him if he wanted water, he often said no. They knew he was dying for water. But if he believed they did not control him, that he was free, then the Viet Cong would stop trying to control him. The desire for water became something he controlled; not them. He would not imagine himself in the state they imagined him in. That, he says, is what got him through eight years of brutal captivity.

Leaders who practice this attitude at crucial times see that the imagination is much more powerful than information. The imagination may be the only true power we have. It cannot be stripped from us no matter how much we gain or lose.

2. *Know how the imagination works.* The most powerful ideas are as simple as ideals. They are clearly expressed. The more concentrated they are, the more powerful. Ronald Reagan could be considered both intellectually empty and a thinking person's radical because his fundamental beliefs were simple and strong. Reagan's big idea—a free market, a free world—was often repeated. His idea that the cold war would end and capitalism would win seemed crazy for years. But what he imagined came to pass. The success of his imagination had everything to do with the fact that everyone knew what he stood for. That's how his idea became larger than life.

Paradoxically, a leader in the service of a big idea becomes greater by becoming smaller: He gains stature by that alliance as he does by no other.

Barry Diller raises more investment money than almost anyone else in media because he's always talking about the future, the fourth network, and the new audiences, more than he talks about technology or numbers. Diller is known as a man of ideas. Ideas invite others to respond with imaginative gusto.

Big imaginative ideas succeed by building on two principles. They are *democratic* (shared by everybody) and *demotic* (like art, they convince by being suggestive, not merely by making rational sense). By being evocative rather than explicit, they invite participation.

In working in the imaginal instead of the rational mind, it is important to leave much unsaid so others can complete the picture on their own. This is different from the notion that others will "buy in" to a vision the leader sets out. The imagination thrives on sketchier ground and creates a deeper common bond to an idea.

3. *Use triggers of the imagination.* Leaders often need to trick themselves in order to turn off their rational mind and reroute their mental energy to their imagination. One technique was a favorite of Winston Churchill's.

Churchill had great respect for information. He wrote a six-volume history of Great Britain. He amassed more facts about the early German arms buildup while he was out of office than England's prime minister had at the time. But his respect for information did not diminish how strongly he emphasized his imagination.

"Energy and poetry sum him up," Clement Attlee said of Churchill. Going beyond the facts at hand proved essential when England was resisting entering another war. Looking weak by all measure of the facts, the country had to be convinced by imaginative leaps that it could win a war.

Churchill used an unusual trigger of the imagination to make that leap. He always wrote two speeches: one in standard prose, in sentences that built into paragraphs. Then he set down the speech in what he called "psalm form" because it looked as though it were being pointed for singing. By arranging his words visually on the page, he brought poetic power to his speeches, lifting the spirit of his listeners in ways that a conventional reading cannot.

Consider what Churchill would see when he glanced down at the final draft of a speech:

> We cannot yet see how deliverance will come
> or when it will come.
> But nothing is more certain
> than every trace of Hitler's foot steps,
> every strain of his infected
> and corroding fingers,
> will be sponged and purged
> and, if need be, blasted
> from the surface of the earth.

Using the white space of the page in this way adds power to the voice. It leaves room for listeners to fill in where the reader may be going, and to go there too. It is a simple technique that allows leaders to go further—not in what they can do, but what they cannot.

A trigger of the imagination is not just aural. It can be visual. Gianni Agnelli, founder of Fiat, did much the same as Churchill, but visually. He once explained his success as follows: Every morning he would take his coffee on his balcony. He would let his eyes drift out to the far horizon. He stared into the distance for a few minutes, then reeled his gaze back to matters at hand: the coffee cup or the newspaper, or a meeting on his agenda. Then he would send his gaze out again to the horizon. A great leader, a veritable Merchant of Light, brings the far perspective into every meeting, and this is what we know as inspiration: providing others a glimpse of the distant horizon. If you as a leader see it, others will see it too.

4. *To know what you think, see what you have to say.* What do you stand for? Every leader stands for something, and to see what idea holds your life in its command is an "aha" of the first order.

Soon after Andy Grove signed a contract for his most recent book, he learned he had prostate cancer. I thought he would postpone writing the book, but he took to it more fiercely. The book, which he came to call *Only the Paranoid Survive*, gave him greater insight into his character, not just his management method. He saw how his whole life was summed up by this phrase, as true for him as a boy trying to escape the Communists in Hungary as it was when he guided Intel through many difficult moments, as when he confronted this crisis in his life. He had recognized the big idea with which he was always aligned. As Grove saw his position expand from CEO to thinker, so others came to see him: Grove became larger than business life.

Writing *Only the Paranoid* Survive may have helped him inch ahead of competitors in being named *Time* magazine's Man of the Year. *Time* editors admitted that Grove was an unusual choice for their honor, given that Intel is hardly a household name and manufactures a product few understand. Writing that book recreated him as a Kissinger-like statesman. Who was *Time*'s second choice? Another thinker, Alan Greenspan, student of Ayn Rand. Greenspan, however, never wrote a book.

Some of the greatest leaders were also writers. Churchill said, "It was my only ambition to be master of the spoken word." He knew that words are deeds. Declare something, and the world shifts. Reality often echoes words, which is why people warn: be careful what you wish for.

5. *Understand that the imagination demands the commitment of your body, not just your mind and soul.* Ted Turner started CNN before there was an audience, before he had the money to keep it afloat longer than six months, and before he had FCC approval of long-term satellite use. What clinched his success in cable was putting his body on the line.

Turner had tried without much luck to sell the premise of CNN. The networks considered bureau feeds good enough. Editors from the *New York Times* laughed at him. "What will your cameras pointed all over the world cover when nothing's happening? Two-bit fires?"

Months before the CNN launch, Turner decided to go ahead and set sail in the America's Cup race. All the boats headed straight into a brutal storm over the Atlantic. Several boats were reported missing or capsized. Fifteen people were killed in what turned out to be the worst disaster in racing history. Daniel Schorr had just left a prestigious post at NBC to join Turner's insane venture. That morning he ran into an old associate from NBC. "Hey, turn on the television: your boss is dead. The news just came in." Schorr's heart nearly stopped. Without Turner, there'd be no CNN. Just then Schorr took a call from Atlanta: Turner was alive. What's more, he'd won the race by outrunning the storm. All the news cameras had been focused on the storm. There were no cameras scanning the periphery.

Schorr put down the phone and told his friend at NBC: "Turner's not dead, but you guys are." Turner had inadvertently become the key marketing pitch for CNN.

The imagination cannot be controlled. To follow the imagination means you will eventually put your body on the line, not just your soul. When you keep a big idea in mind, say it and live it, then you become like a soldier in your own army. Body, soul, and mind work toward the same end. Your job then is not to get in your own way. It is to treat every surprise not as something to be controlled but to be accorded the respect you would show an uninvited guest.

The Brazen Age

Making these habits part of a leadership repertoire makes one comfortable with big ideas and imaginative agendas. One feels unconstrained by the available facts. The possibilities become endless. Leadership starts to feel exciting again.

Steve Ross, who began his career managing parking lots and eventually built the entertainment megalith that became Time Warner, was something of a modern-day Merchant of Light. He often told the following story:

"When I was a teenager and my father was dying, he gave me the best advice possible. He said, there are three categories of people in this world. The first is the individual who wakes up in the morning and goes into the office and proceeds to dream. The second category is the individual who gets up in the morning, goes into the office, and proceeds to work 16 hours a day. The third is the individual who comes into the office, dreams for about an hour, and then proceeds to do something about his dreams.

"He said, 'Go into the third category for only one reason: there's no competition.'" Ross dreamed big and acted on what he imagined—Churchill's formula of poetry and energy. Ross, says his biographer, "exemplified a lived art," always over the top. As a result, people loved working for Ross. His big ideas, his love of surprise, his brand of Churchill-like dreams enabled him to create something far bigger than numbers or intellect would say was possible.

Four centuries after Bacon wrote about the Merchants of Light, Marshall McLuhan drew a valuable distinction between *learning* and *knowing*. All work would become "paid learning," predicted McLuhan, which has come to pass. Leaders, then, have to distinguish themselves by knowing. Imagination is knowing: sensing, suspecting, seeing into the darkness where all new things begin, just as our world was born out of darkness. McLuhan himself said that light was the purest form of knowledge. Having no characteristics itself, it enables others to see. To be a Merchant of Light is to have few limits and vast advantages. It is to be able to penetrate everywhere, even darkness, and be bound by nothing.

Harriet Rubin, former editor of Doubleday/Currency, published some of the most influential business books of the decade, including 40 best-sellers. She now speaks widely and writes for the *Wall Street Journal, Fast Company,* and other business publications. She is author of *The Princessa: Machiavelli for Women* and *Soloing: Realizing Your Life's Ambitions*.

Index

Leader to Leader

*A quarterly publication of
the Drucker Foundation
and Jossey-Bass Publishers*
Frances Hesselbein,
Editor-in-Chief

Leader to Leader is a unique management
publication, a quarterly report on management,
leadership, and strategy written by today's top
leaders *themselves*. Four times a year, *Leader to
Leader* keeps you ahead of the curve by bringing
you the latest offerings from a peerless selection
of world-class executives, best-selling management authors, leading consultants, and respected social thinkers, making *Leader to Leader* unlike any other
magazine or professional publication today.

Think of it as a short, intensive seminar with today's top thinkers and doers—
people like Peter F. Drucker, Rosabeth Moss Kanter, Max De Pree, Charles
Handy, Esther Dyson, Stephen Covey, Meg Wheatley, Peter Senge, and others.

Subscriptions to **Leader to Leader** are $199.00.
501(c)(3) nonprofit organizations can subscribe for $99.00 (must supply tax-exempt
ID number when subscribing). Prices subject to change without notice.

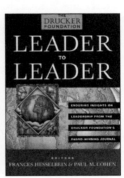

Leader to Leader

*Enduring Insights on Leadership from the
Drucker Foundation's Award-Winning Journal*
Frances Hesselbein, Paul M. Cohen, Editors

The world's thought leaders come together in
Leader to Leader, an inspiring examination of
mission, leadership, values, innovation, building
collaborations, shaping effective institutions, and
creating community. Management pioneer Peter F.
Drucker; Southwest Airlines CEO Herb Kelleher;
best-selling authors Warren Bennis, Stephen R.
Covey, and Charles Handy; Pulitzer Prize winner
Doris Kearns Goodwin; Harvard professors Rosabeth Moss Kanter and Regina
Herzlinger; and learning organization expert Peter Senge are among those who
share their knowledge and experience in this essential resource. Their essays
will spark ideas, open doors, and inspire all those who face the challenge of
leading in an ever-changing environment.

For a reader's guide, see www.leaderbooks.org

Hardcover   ISBN 0-7879-4726-1 $27.00

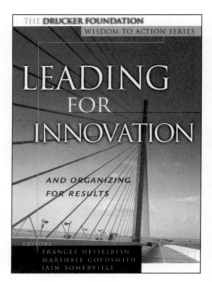

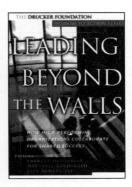

Leading Beyond the Walls

Frances Hesselbein, Marshall Goldsmith,
Iain Somerville, Editors

from the Drucker Foundation's Wisdom to Action Series

"There is need for acceptance on the part of leaders in every single institution, and in every single sector, that they, as leaders, have two responsibilities. They are responsible and accountable for the performance of their institution, and that has to be concentrated, focused, limited. They are responsible however, also, for the community as a whole. This requires commitment. It requires willingness to accept that other institutions have different values, respect for these values, and willingness to learn what these values are. It requires hard work. But above all, it requires commitment; conviction; dedication to the Common Good. Yes, each institution is autonomous and has to do its own work the way each instrument in an orchestra plays its own part. But there is also the 'score,' the community. And only if the individual instrument contributes to the score is there music. Otherwise there is only noise. This book is about the score."

—Peter F. Drucker

Increasingly, leaders and their organizations work in ways that extend beyond the walls of the enterprise. These partnerships, alliances, and networks allow organizations to achieve new levels of performance. At the same time, they create new challenges. Leaders "beyond the walls" must be adept at building and maintaining relationships, comfortable in working with individuals and organizations they cannot control, and able to move beyond the old preconceptions.

Leading Beyond the Walls presents insights from over twenty-five thought leaders from all three sectors, exploring the challenges and opportunities of partnership as well as the unique practices and perspectives that have helped individuals and organizations become more effective.

Paperback   ISBN 0-7879-5555-8 $16.50

The Drucker Foundation Future Series

All Three Volumes in a Slipcover Case
Boxed Set   ISBN 0-7879-4696-6 $80.00
Paperback Set ISBN 0-7879-5370-9 $49.00

Business Week Best-Seller!
The Leader of the Future
**New Visions, Strategies, and Practices
for the Next Era**
Frances Hesselbein, Marshall Goldsmith,
Richard Beckhard, Editors

World-class contributors offer insights into
the future quality of our lives, businesses, organizations, society, and the leadership required to
move us into the exciting unknown.

Hardcover   ISBN 0-7879-0180-6 $26.00
Paperback   ISBN 0-7879-0935-1 $18.00

Now in Paperback!
The Organization of the Future
Frances Hesselbein, Marshall Goldsmith, Richard Beckhard, Editors

"Required reading. If you don't use this book to help guide your organization
through the changes, you may well be left behind."   *—Nonprofit World*

Hardcover   ISBN 0-7879-0303-5 $26.00
Paperback   ISBN 0-7879-5203-6 $18.00

Now in Paperback!
The Community of the Future
Frances Hesselbein, Marshall Goldsmith, Richard Beckhard,
Richard F. Schubert, Editors

"This book of essays is full of rampant idealism. Its authors share a desire to
better the world through their ideas and actions."   *—Christian Science Monitor*

Hardcover   ISBN 0-7879-1006-6 $26.00
Paperback   ISBN 0-7879-5204-4 $18.00

FAX	**CALL**	**MAIL**	**WEB**
Toll Free	Toll Free	Jossey-Bass Publishers	Secure ordering at:
24 hours a day:	6am to 5pm PST:	989 Market St.	www.josseybass.com
800-605-2665	800-956-7739	San Francisco, CA 94105-1741	

Leading in a Time of Change

A conversation between Peter F. Drucker and Peter M. Senge

Peter F. Drucker, Peter M. Senge, and Frances Hesselbein

Sit at the table with the visionary leaders who are setting the agenda for organizational leadership and change.

The Drucker Foundation presents a conversation with Peter F. Drucker and Peter M. Senge, hosted by Frances Hesselbein. In this dynamic package—which includes a video and companion workbook—two great minds of modern management share their wisdom on how leaders can prepare themselves and their organizations for the inevitable changes that lie ahead.

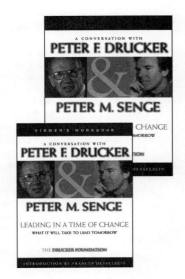

Watch the video and witness a remarkable conversation between Peter Drucker and Peter Senge as they talk about the importance of learning to lead change for all organizations. Using the principles presented in this stimulating video and workbook, you can help transform your organization into a change leader. In their discussion Drucker and Senge reveal how you can:

- Develop systematic methods to look for and anticipate change.

- Focus on and invest in opportunities rather than problems.

- Phase out established products and services.

- Balance change and continuity.

- Motivate and retain top performers and create a mind-set among employees that embraces positive change.

The companion workbook will be an invaluable aid in making strategic decisions. It will also serve as a fundamental resource for planning and implementing changes within your organization. This extraordinary package is an ideal tool for executive retreats, management training, and personal leadership development.

42-minute video with companion Viewer's Workbook ISBN 0-7879-5603-1 $195.00

FAX
Toll Free
24 hours a day:
800-605-2665

CALL
Toll Free
6am to 5pm PST:
800-956-7739

MAIL
Jossey-Bass Publishers
989 Market St.
San Francisco, CA 94105-1741

WEB
Secure ordering at:
www.josseybass.com

Lessons in Leadership
Peter F. Drucker

Over the span of his sixty-year career, Peter F. Drucker has worked with many exemplary leaders in the nonprofit sector, government, and business. In the course of his work, he has observed these leaders closely and learned from them the attributes of effective leadership. In this video, Drucker presents inspirational portraits of five outstanding leaders, showing how each brought different strengths to the task, and shares the lessons we can learn from their approaches to leadership. Drucker's insights (plus the accompanying *Facilitator's Guide* and *Workbook*) will help participants identify which methods work best for them and how to recognize their own particular strengths in leadership.

1 20-minute video + 1 *Facilitator's Guide* + 1 *Workbook*
ISBN 0-7879-4497-1 $95.00

Excellence in Nonprofit Leadership
Peter F. Drucker, Max De Pree, Frances Hesselbein

This video package is a powerful three-in-one development program for building more effective nonprofit organizations and boards. *Excellence in Nonprofit Leadership* presents three modules that can be used independently or sequentially to help nonprofit boards and staff strengthen leadership throughout the organization. The video contains three twenty-minute programs: (I) *Lessons in Leadership* with Peter Drucker (as described above); (II) *Identifying the Needs of Followers*, with Max De Pree and Michele Hunt; and (III) *Leading Through Mission*, with Frances Hesselbein. The video comes with one *Facilitator's Guide*, which contains complete instructions for leading all three programs, and one free *Workbook*, which is designed to help participants deepen and enrich the learning experience.

1 60-minute video + 1 *Facilitator's Guide* + 1 *Workbook*
ISBN 0-7879-4496-3 $140.00